JUL

P9-CBX-181

THE
UNIVERSITY
WE NEED

THE UNIVERSITY WE NEED

Reforming American Higher Education

Warren Treadgold

ENCOUNTER BOOKS
New York • London

First American edition published in 2018 by Encounter Books,
an activity of Encounter for Culture and Education, Inc.,
a nonprofit, tax exempt corporation.
Encounter Books website address: www.encounterbooks.com

Manufactured in the United States and printed on
acid-free paper. The paper used in this publication meets
the minimum requirements of ANSI/NISO Z39.48–1992
(R 1997) (*Permanence of Paper*).

FIRST AMERICAN EDITION

LIBRARY OF CONGRESS CATALOGING-IN-PUBLICATION DATA
Library of Congress Cataloging-in-Publication Data

Names: Treadgold, Warren, 1949– author.
Title: The university we need : reforming American higher education /
Warren Treadgold.
Description: New York : Encounter Books, [2018] |
Includes bibliographical references and index.
Identifiers: LCCN 2017039031 (print) | LCCN 2017059578 (ebook) |
ISBN 9781594039904 (Ebook) | ISBN 9781594039898 (hardback : alk. paper)
Subjects: LCSH: Education, Higher—Aims and objectives—United States. |
Educational change—United States.
Classification: LCC LA227.4 (ebook) | LCC LA227.4 .T375 2018 (print) |
DDC 378.73—dc23
LC record available at https://lccn.loc.gov/2017039031
Interior page design and composition: BooksByBruce.com

To the many fine scholars
who have left the academic profession
over the past fifty years in disgust or despair

CONTENTS

PREFACE

This book is more candid than most books written about higher education by professors. Even professors who know that something is seriously wrong are usually reluctant to criticize the college or university where they work, at least until they have a chance to leave, or to make negative statements that apply to most or all colleges or universities. Criticizing your own institution not only can offend your colleagues and embarrass your students but also can hurt the reputation of the whole community in which you live. Being an outspoken critic of most or all universities can also hurt your chances of finding another job. On the other hand, if no one speaks out, the resulting silence can become a sort of academic *omertà*, giving outsiders the false impression that all is well, or at least not so terribly bad, and leaving the task of criticizing higher education to commentators who have little understanding of it. This is one reason that almost all of the many recent books about the problems of higher education fail to make specific or practical proposals for improving it: the insiders are unwilling to propose shaking things up very much, and the outsiders have no clear idea of what needs to be done. In reading many of those books, most of which are longer than this one, I have found few if any proposals as specific and feasible as those suggested here.

Some readers will probably think these proposals are too big and ambitious to be feasible. Many smaller and less ambitious proposals have been tried, yet American colleges and universities have grown steadily worse. By now the problems are too large and too deeply ingrained for modest solutions to make any significant difference, and American higher education has deteriorated so badly that it cannot be expected to reform itself from within. This means that the best hope is for outside intervention, either from enlightened federal legislation or from enlightened donors, or both. For those of us who hope for such intervention, in some respects the sorry state of higher education today is an advantage: the need for change has become glaring, while the system has grown so troubled and confused that it is vulnerable to new ideas and would have trouble fighting reform legislation. To propose enlisting the help of a relatively small group of sympathetic legislators and donors seems far more realistic than to propose changing the minds of millions of unsympathetic professors and administrators.

Since detailed descriptions of what is wrong can already be found in several good books that I cite, like Richard Arum and Josipa Roksa's *Academically Adrift*, the present book consists primarily of analysis and prescriptions. Its intended readership is anyone who thinks that colleges and universities matter and who is ready to consider the possibility that they could be made better. I have made my suggested improvements reasonably specific and concrete, even if some of the details could doubtless be improved upon, because I want to show how something could be done about problems that many people think are hopeless.

My best thanks go to Joseph Epstein for his help and advice on this whole project, and to the *Weekly Standard*, the *Wilson Quarterly*, *Academic Questions*, and *Commentary* for publishing earlier versions of chapters 3, 4, 6, and 7 and for granting me permission to include revised and expanded versions of them here.

Saint Louis, Missouri
New Year's Day 2018

Chapter 1

DO UNIVERSITIES MATTER?

The Power of Universities

Although many people think the Left has won the culture wars for good, few wars end in a total and permanent victory for one side. The Left's dominance is recent, and shows signs of being insecure. After eight years of the mostly leftist presidency of Barack Obama, a Gallup poll showed 72 percent of Americans were dissatisfied with the state of the country; the last time the poll showed a satisfied majority was in 2004, under George W. Bush.[1] After defeating Democrats who took largely leftist positions in 2016, Republicans now control the presidency, Congress, and most state governments. While the Supreme Court remains divided, another Republican appointment could soon give it its first majority of strict constructionists since judicial activism began in the sixties. Conservative think tanks and foundations are now at least as influential as their left-leaning counterparts. As for religion, some strong conservative voices can be found among orthodox Catholics, evangelical Protestants, and Orthodox Jews. Though the Left retains a clear advantage in the national media, opponents of the Left can now reach a wide audience through Fox News, talk radio, and a range of conservative journals and websites. Among celebrities, whose influence on our culture has increased, the Left also holds a clear advantage, but the Right has its own influential celebrities, one of whom is now President. As of now, the only major center of influence where the Left is overwhelmingly dominant is the university.

Universities are now the most important source of ideas for American leftism, which first emerged from the student radicalism of the sixties. For almost forty years, especially after the crushing defeat of the student-supported George McGovern in the 1972 presidential election, most Democratic politicians—and liberal media and think tanks—remained uncomfortable with student leftism. As presidents, Jimmy Carter and Bill Clinton often tried to appease leftists but avoided pursuing leftist policies that looked unpopular, as most leftist policies then did. The less cautious leftism of Michael Dukakis was probably the main reason he lost the 1988 presidential election so decisively. But during all this time the leftist presence in universities steadily grew, especially among professors but also among the students they taught. Professors and students became more active in politics, mostly as organizers but sometimes as candidates, and made their voices heard in the media. Even in solidly Republican states, Democratic candidates could count on strong support in college and university towns. Support from students and professors made a major contribution to the presidential campaign of Barack Obama, a former lecturer at the University of Chicago Law School.

In 2016 campus leftists had a presidential candidate who agreed with almost all of their views: Bernie Sanders. Significantly, Sanders called himself a socialist, not a Democrat, and campaigned on proposals that the government relieve student debts and pay full tuition for students at public universities. The influence of university students, recent graduates, and professors in Democratic primaries was a major reason that Sanders came close to winning the nomination, though he had little support within the Democratic Party organization and was running against Hillary Clinton, who had the organization firmly behind her. While campaigning for the nomination, Sanders forced Clinton to move to the Left and even to adopt a slightly modified form of his proposal for free tuition at public universities, despite the misgivings she had expressed earlier about its high cost. In the general election campaign, she ran on a platform much like that of Sanders. Though college students, professors, and administrators strongly opposed Trump and favored Clinton, her acceptance of their ideology was probably a key reason she lost the election. Conversely, Trump's rejection of that ideology was probably a key reason he won, with particularly strong support from voters without college degrees.[2]

A recent poll showed that 58 percent of Republicans and "Republican-leaning independents" think "colleges and universities have a negative effect on the way things are going in the country."[3] Another poll reported that 75 percent of Republicans and 66 percent of all Americans think colleges and universities are not doing "enough to ensure that students are exposed to a wide variety of viewpoints."[4] Yet even some of those who recognize the leftist dominance in universities may be tempted not to worry too much about it. After all, campus leftism failed to prevail in the recent election, even against an unpopular Republican candidate. Universities also seem not to be essential as a source of political ideas. Conservative think tanks have shown that they can prepare sophisticated political agendas outside universities. Conservative journalists, some of them also connected with think tanks, can perform similar functions. In fact, conservative think tanks and journals have developed a wider range of ideas on trade, immigration, taxation, foreign policy, and other issues than leftists will tolerate on campus. These conservative ideas have also proved more popular than campus leftism, which insists on berating large numbers of voters for their supposed racism, sexism, and other prejudices. In the presidential campaign Clinton expressed her pride at having made Republicans her enemies, denounced many Trump supporters as "deplorables," and lectured orthodox Christians and Orthodox Jews on how they needed to change their supposedly bigoted moral beliefs. These positions, which alienated some people who disliked Trump and might otherwise have voted for Clinton, were a direct result of the leftist dogma making it a moral imperative to defend the allegedly oppressed against their alleged oppressors.

Despite the success of campus leftism in mobilizing student opinion first behind Sanders and then behind Clinton, some people still think the universities' influence has been overstated. After all, many university alumni of conservative or moderate views have been exposed to campus leftism without embracing it, and some of them have reacted strongly against it. Then too, America has a few universities and colleges that dissent from the leftist consensus, such as Baylor University, Ave Maria University, and Hillsdale College, where students can go to avoid leftist propaganda. Besides, even some very left-wing universities have a few professors who are moderate or even conservative and influence some students. Even though opportunities for conservatives and moderates to pursue graduate study are severely limited, and their chances of being hired as professors are even slimmer, why would any non-leftist want to be a professor anyway? Regular academic job openings are few, and academic salaries are low.

Nobody really thinks we can get rid of universities altogether, but many conservatives think we should try to marginalize them as much as possible. Conservative governors and legislatures have been cutting spending on state universities for years. The consequences include large increases in tuition, corresponding increases in student debt, and administrative attempts to reduce costs by offering online courses and hiring adjunct professors, regardless of the effect on the quality of instruction. Lavish spending on buildings and athletics persists, because students and donors like such things and no university wants to lose tuition or donations. Administrative costs also continue to soar, often to the point of surpassing spending on teaching, because administrators are the ones who make the budgetary decisions. And because leftism has become so dominant on campus, those who profess it are still hired as regular faculty, to the exclusion of others. Thus black, queer, and feminist studies are sacrosanct, while Shakespeare and the American Revolution are mentioned, if at all, in courses on women and slavery as examples of sexism and racism. Meanwhile, the growing problem of student debt is being used in a campaign for government forgiveness of the debt, which would just be a belated and indirect way of paying the original tuition and increasing government spending on universities.

The results of the 2016 election are likely to reinforce these trends. Many faculty and administrators take Trump's views and temperament as proof of their belief that conservatism is inevitably bigoted and anti-intellectual. Though a Trump administration may curb federal efforts to make universities try accused rapists in kangaroo courts or enforce affirmative action in admissions and hiring, most university administrators are happy to pursue such policies without any government compulsion. In 2000, the last time Republicans took both the presidency and Congress, campus leftists worked harder than ever to consolidate their control, sometimes arguing that it was needed to balance Republican dominance of government. (Yet nobody seems to have thought that the Democrats' winning the presidency and Congress in 2008 meant that universities should hire more Republicans.) Since then universities have become steadily more hostile to conservatives and moderates.[5] Every year many more professors with conservative or moderate views retire than are hired. The few remaining conservative and moderate professors, having already learned to keep quiet on campus because speaking out only inflames leftist opposition, now appear even more reluctant to speak because most of them dislike Trump and fear being identified with him.[6] No matter what happens in electoral politics, conservatives and moderates seem to become ever more marginalized in universities.

Relations between universities and the federal government are now more openly hostile than ever before. Conservatives in Congress have come up with several measures that would affect universities, none of which is likely to help. One idea is a law requiring the richest universities to spend more of the income from their endowments. Such a law, while annoying universities that love to hoard large endowments as a matter of prestige, would probably result in their spending more not on teaching but on administration, buildings, athletics, and leftist indoctrination. Another idea, considered by Republicans as part of the 2017 tax reform act but eventually dropped, is to tax as income the tuition that universities remit for most of their graduate students. Without raising any significant revenue, that tax would impose important debts on graduate students, most of whom are already in debt, poorly paid, overworked, and unlikely ever to get regular academic jobs. One proposal actually included in the 2017 tax reform is an excise tax of 1.4 percent on the income from university endowments of more than $500,000 per student. This tax, which again will raise no significant revenue but is supposed to encourage reductions in tuition, will be only a minor irritation to the few elite colleges and universities that Congress wants to penalize. Bernie Sanders, however, to the annoyance of the majority leader of the Senate, Mitch McConnell, managed to use a Senate rule to apply the excise tax to a small and rather conservative college in Kentucky that offers its low-income students free tuition.[7] Such measures, like cutting state funding for universities, are apparently designed more to rebuke them than to reform them.

Many conservatives seem to take an attitude toward higher education much like their attitude toward government. Since neither education nor government can be eliminated entirely, they think that both should be limited and intimidated. Yet turning your back on institutions you dislike leaves them to be run by people you dislike; and trying to force people you dislike to do things you want usually fails. Blind hatred against Washington can result in nominating unelectable candidates, antagonizing competent officials who might otherwise pass good laws and repeal bad ones, and reinforcing leftist arguments that conservatives hate not just bad government but government itself. Hatred of universities can result in ignoring real possibilities for reform, imposing cuts that harm teaching and research without reducing leftist indoctrination, and reinforcing leftist arguments that conservatives are hostile not just to leftism but to education itself. Just as term limits usually lead to electing state legislators who are less competent but no less leftist (the California legislature is a prime example), abolishing tenure for professors would almost certainly lead to leftist administrators' hiring even less competent and more leftist professors. Conservatives should rather be trying to encourage and support conservatives and moderates who want to become or remain professors. Conservatives will suffer along with everybody else if reduced funding damages universities' research, especially in medicine and the sciences, and leaves future generations badly educated and poorly prepared for the workforce.

While the 2016 election was a defeat for campus leftism, Trump's victory was hardly a victory for conservative intellectuals, most of whom wanted other candidates and opposed many of Trump's policies. Moreover, no thoughtful observer can feel confident that the 2016 election will begin a long period of conservative dominance over American government. Republican and Libertarian presidential and congressional candidates won only narrow majorities of votes in 2016, even if the Electoral College and congressional district boundaries produced comfortable Republican majorities. Amateur politicians like Trump have had a poor record of success in executive office in American states and foreign countries, and Trump's approval ratings have been consistently low and steadily sinking since the beginning of his presidency. Professional Republican politicians, even though most of them never liked Trump, will probably share the blame with him if his presidency founders. Just as in 2016 many voters were ready to dismiss their misgivings about Trump out of dislike for Hillary Clinton, so by 2018 or 2020 many voters may be ready to dismiss their misgivings about Democratic candidates out of dislike for Trump.

Though campus leftism was probably an electoral disadvantage for Democrats in 2016, it may prove less disadvantageous in future elections. For one thing, sensitivity to charges of racism has already become a durable feature of American politics. No white politician with Barack Obama's thin record would have been nominated and elected President in 2008.[8] Although Obamacare, Obama's main legislative accomplishment, was consistently unpopular and contributed to losses for Democrats in congressional elections after it was passed, Obama himself was reelected handily in 2012. The same polls that showed public disapproval of the condition of the country and of Obamacare showed much more approval of Obama's performance as President, which was near 60 percent by the end of his term.[9] In 2012 and 2016, Republican primary voters showed surprising enthusiasm for two poorly qualified black candidates, Herman Cain and Ben Carson. Many Americans remain uncertain that the shooting of Michael Brown in Ferguson in 2014 was justified (as even the Obama Justice Department conceded it was) or that charges of widespread police brutality against blacks are exaggerated, as seems clearly to be the case. The obvious explanation for these anomalies in public opinion is that many voters want to avoid expressing any hint of bias against anyone black.

Most voters are more comfortable with rejecting leftist charges that Americans are oppressing women, Hispanics, and Muslims. Having had the experience either of being women themselves or of knowing some women very well, most voters dismissed the idea that sexism was the only possible reason for voting against such a flawed candidate as Hillary Clinton, or even for opposing abortion. (While most voters are concerned about sexual harassment, Hillary Clinton was unable to exploit charges of Trump's harassment of women because she had so stridently defended her husband against similar charges.) Most Americans also reject the idea that xenophobia is the only possible reason for wanting to limit immigration or that Islamophobia is the only possible reason for fearing Islamic terrorism. Yet campus leftists, with strong support within the Democratic Party, still insist on the prevalence of racism, sexism, xenophobia, and Islamophobia. Since leftist professors and university administrators have been intensifying their indoctrination of their students, who are a growing share of the electorate, leftism is likely to spread further in American politics, as it already has among younger voters.

Outside universities, conservative think tanks and media have done solid work in combating the growth of leftism. Today conservatives are in a much stronger position nationwide than they were before they launched *National Review* in 1955, the Heritage Foundation in 1973, or Fox News in 1996. Each of these initiatives inspired the creation of new conservative foundations and media, while promoting conservative influence over previously existing foundations and media. Conservative think tanks, journals, radio, and television now strongly influence the Republican Party and play a major role in American political and cultural life. Yet they cannot or will not do some things that universities can. Political journals and think tanks tend to hire committed partisans and are therefore more hospitable to leftists or conservatives than they are to moderates or pragmatists, or to specialists in fields not closely related to politics. Universities hire a wide range of specialists and can claim (if often falsely) to hire less partisan scholars. Moreover, only universities can give comprehensive training to future generations of thinkers and researchers. People who expect that conservative think tanks and media will be able to go on recruiting enough talented university graduates indefinitely probably underestimate how far to the left universities have moved.

In theory, think tanks and journals could grant tenure to a number of researchers and allow them freedom to develop their research and ideas regardless of deadlines, ideology, or relevance to current affairs. In practice, understandably, conservative think tanks and journals have a limited tolerance for results that take a long time, diverge from orthodox conservatism, or adopt a perspective of centuries or millennia. We should therefore not expect conservative think tanks or journals to produce thoroughly researched studies explaining, for example, how the internal flaws of Communism caused it to fail, why Shakespeare is an author everyone should know, or that climate engineering is a realistic solution to global warming. Even if conservatives outside universities write such articles or books, they will be ignored by most professional academics, because the academic consensus is that Communism failed because of unfortunate accidents, Shakespeare was just another oppressive white male, and reducing carbon emissions is the only possible solution to global warming. Professional academics assume that conservatives arrive at conservative conclusions regardless of the evidence, while universities are supposed to arrive at the truth and to be free to pursue it wherever they find it. Yet universities have shown none of the growth of conservative influence apparent in think tanks, media, and national politics.

Years of calling attention to the growth of campus leftism and forming organizations to resist it have proved insufficient to reverse its progress. Books and articles describing the tightening grip of the Left on campus have appeared frequently at least since Allan Bloom's bestselling *The Closing of the American Mind* in 1987, if not since William Buckley's *God and Man at Yale* in 1951.[10] Campus organizations dedicated to defending academic freedom against leftists include the Intercollegiate Studies Institute (ISI), founded in 1953; the National Association of Scholars (NAS), founded in 1987; the Foundation for Individual Rights in Education (FIRE), founded in 1999; and Heterodox Academy, founded in 2015. In early 2016 the University of Chicago issued a statement of Principles on Freedom of Expression that unequivocally defended academic freedom against recent challenges. Recently even some decidedly liberal commentators, like Nicholas Kristof and Frank Bruni of the *New York Times*, have expressed alarm about the monolithic leftism of American universities. (Bruni's eyes seem to have been opened after he wrote in a column how he had been "transformed" by a wonderful college course on Shakespeare, only to receive an email from his old teacher lamenting that her sort of course had been replaced by the likes of "Global Feminisms.")[11] Nonetheless, campus leftism continues to advance.

Universities at an Impasse

By now not even protecting academic freedom can ensure a real diversity of ideas in our universities. The dominant ideology on campus asserts that ideas cannot be objectively right or wrong but are either just or unjust, depending on whether they serve to enforce the oppression of allegedly oppressed identity groups or to combat such oppression. Thus, for instance, no combination of evidence or arguments can justify the conclusion that American law enforcement is not racist—that a white policeman shot a black criminal in self-defense is an unacceptable excuse. We must even exclude evidence or arguments that enforcing laws against black criminals benefits most black citizens by protecting them from crime. According to leftist dogma, even if such statements can be proved by ostensibly objective criteria, they are still unjustifiable, because they serve to reinforce the hegemony of a racist white power structure over an oppressed black minority. We cannot even object to the oppression of a law-abiding black majority by a criminal black minority, because oppression can only be attributed to white oppressors, not to a subgroup of the black oppressed. In these and other cases of alleged racism, sexism, and other forms of bias, free speech and open debate are seen simply as instruments of oppression.

The dominant leftist opinion considers fighting racism, sexism, and other forms of oppression to be so vital that it supersedes everything else. The only argument needed to reject any work of scholarship, literature, or art is to allege bias somewhere in it toward some oppressed group, regardless of the work's scholarly, literary, or artistic merits. A simple assertion that something said or written offends supposedly oppressed groups is enough to discredit it, even if the speaker or author meant no offense by it and most members of the group take no offense at it. In fact, since scholarly, literary, or artistic merits are considered far less interesting than leftist ideas of social justice, most literature and art are considered uninteresting, along with most scholarship on subjects apart from leftist ideas of social justice. Thus universities have lost interest in teaching great literature and art, empirical knowledge, and critical thinking, which used to be considered the main function of universities. Instead our universities want to teach only leftist writings and ideas, most of them very recent, while teaching other writings and ideas only as examples of oppression that should be condemned. Speech and debate are increasingly limited to identifying and vilifying new forms of supposed oppression of minorities. Many universities enforce such views through "bias report teams" that investigate alleged bias among their students and faculty.[12]

Under such ground rules, arguing with campus leftists is practically useless, and if leftists control a campus, free speech there cannot be much more than nominal. Campus leftists now regard the social and cultural views of conservatives and moderates in much the same way as most of us regard Holocaust denial. To honor the principle of free speech, we let Holocaust deniers speak, but we pay no real attention to any evidence or arguments they allege, which we dismiss as motivated by anti-Semitism, not by an interest in the truth. We would oppose hiring them as professors, unless they taught subjects unrelated to the Holocaust and never mentioned their views on the Holocaust in the classroom. We expect pertinent college courses to mention that Holocaust deniers have existed and still exist but we identify them as examples of prejudice, not as purveyors of a theory worth serious consideration. Campus leftists now apply this kind of thinking to almost all thought, literature, or scholarship that is not leftist. They therefore feel justified in rejecting conservatives and moderates who apply for professorships and excluding conservatives and moderates as guest lecturers or commencement speakers.

Admittedly, most professors would be reluctant to endorse current leftist doctrine in quite as explicit a form as I have described it here. Yet a great many professors follow such a doctrine in practice, and relatively few show any clear preference for academic freedom over leftist ideas of social justice. A recent survey of attitudes about academic freedom sent to the whole faculty at Columbia University received replies from 319 professors, of whom (significantly) 203 identified themselves as Democrats and only 7 as Republicans.[13] After summarizing the responses to questions about how the university should deal with a series of "situations" that raised issues of academic freedom, the surveyors concluded, perhaps too cautiously,

> If an erosion of the norms of academic freedom and free inquiry has taken place at American universities and colleges, it may well be the result of abridgements of the freedom of speech that we have seen on university campuses over the past several decades....The unwillingness to accept the idea that speakers have a right to hurt others' feelings and offend their sensibilities may lead faculty members to think of academic freedom and free inquiry as just another value of the university without any special place among this hierarchy of values. This devaluation, if confirmed by additional research, could have dangerous consequences for the university, including a greater willingness among faculty and students to limit free discourse and free research inquiry.[14]

What can be done? No doubt our courts and legislatures should try to defend the few remaining conservative and moderate speakers and professors on campus against leftist attacks. Voters or alumni can sometimes compel universities to invite conservative or moderate guest lecturers or commencement speakers. We should not, however, expect such guest lecturers, commencement speakers, or professors to begin a free exchange of ideas, even if student and faculty demonstrators allow them to speak. Most of the few professors and administrators who now defend conservative or moderate speakers argue that the speakers' views are indeed noxious but that students should be exposed to them in order to learn how to refute them. Under such circumstances, speakers cannot possibly receive a fair hearing. Some people have suggested an "affirmative action" program to hire conservative professors; but this would be opposed by most conservative academics, who dislike all affirmative action programs. Even if affirmative action for conservatives were imposed on hostile faculties and administrations, the result would probably be a marginalized cohort of second-class professors, in some cases deliberately chosen because they were poorly qualified and likely to discredit conservatism.

In the same way, if a leftist university creates a special conservative college or program, as is sometimes proposed and occasionally done, the result is likely to be an unpopular and underfunded academic ghetto for a few isolated faculty and students. This sort of program can only exist on the sufferance of university administrators who are hostile to its aims and have no interest in its success, because that success would attract attention to the defects of the rest of the university. To the extent that such a program provided a real alternative, it would probably become a focus for student and faculty protesters from the rest of the university. More likely, it would resemble the dummy "democratic" parties that exist as window dressing in Communist China and once existed in Communist Bulgaria and East Germany, designed to give an impression of diversity of opinion without the reality. On the other hand, a body that was completely independent of the university administration but nominally part of the university would have little or no effect on the university's intellectual life, like the Hoover Institution, which is physically located on the Stanford campus but has almost no other connection with Stanford.

As of now, any general effort to recruit conservative graduate students would be irresponsible and futile, given their poor prospects for satisfactory careers in a hostile environment. No doubt a few extremely discreet conservatives and moderates can survive in some of today's leftist universities. But they must be careful never to say anything to colleagues, students, or administrators that differs significantly from leftist orthodoxy and should be ready to lie about their opinions if cornered. (They should also be careful never to donate money to anti-leftist causes, candidates, or political parties, since such donations are a matter of public record.) They should never publish research that disagrees significantly with leftist orthodoxy. Even so, they should be prepared to have their research dismissed as uninteresting because it fails to affirm leftist orthodoxy, and as a result they can hope only for very limited success in their academic careers. Even if for some reason this sort of academic career satisfies them, on campus they will have absolutely no impact in combating leftism or promoting conservative or moderate ideas. A number of such professors can be found today, and they contribute nothing to real intellectual diversity in universities.[15]

Our few conservative colleges and even fewer conservative universities are intellectually unequal to the task of opposing leftism in academia. Especially because most of them emphasize teaching and downplay research, their faculties include only a handful of distinguished scholars and thinkers. Such institutions sometimes give their students a good basic education, but they also confer degrees that offer many fewer opportunities than those of elite institutions. I once taught at Hillsdale College, and though I occasionally hear reports that it has improved since then, in my time it concentrated its efforts not on education, which it often provided on a level barely higher than that of a high school, but on publicity campaigns addressed to conservatives off campus, which it continues today. To most academics and most of the public, our conservative colleges and universities are almost invisible. None is put (or belongs) in anywhere near the same category as Harvard, Stanford, Swarthmore, or Amherst. No conservative college or university has any significant impact on American higher education, national media, or public opinion.

Of course some of our major universities are better than others. The University of Chicago has a comparatively strong (though in recent years

weakened) academic curriculum, and its statement on academic freedom is a rare sign of hope for free speech and thought in contemporary
higher education. Unfortunately, the Chicago faculty displays all the
usual academic obsessions with oppressed race, class, and gender groups.
The university maintains both a "Center for Identity and Inclusion"
and a "Bias Response Team" that investigate reports of allegedly biased
speech and actions; none of this should have any place in a truly free
university.[16] The University of Chicago cannot be expected to defend the
principle that truth has an objective existence independent of doctrines
of oppression, or to train or hire any significant number of conservative
or moderate professors. Most of our Catholic universities are even worse,
including Georgetown and Notre Dame, which have administrations so
determined to win the favor of leftist academic opinion that they barely
bother to disguise their hostility to their minorities of orthodox Catholic
faculty and students.[17]

As I shall explain later in this book, I think the best hope of escaping
this impasse would be the foundation of a major new university, which
could have an impact similar to the establishment of *National Review*
for journals, the Heritage Foundation for think tanks, and Fox News
for television and radio. America has enough conservatives and libertarians with enough money to found a major new university if they choose
to do it. As of now, the prospect of real academic freedom, salaries
based on merit, and a stimulating intellectual community could attract
enough distinguished conservative and moderate academics, including
some distinguished writers and researchers from outside academia, to
staff a major university of about a thousand professors. Such a faculty
could be so brilliant that it would easily outshine the dreary specialists
in race, class, and gender at other major universities, and it should win
admiration outside higher education and grudging respect within it. The
professors of this university would then have enough time before they
retired or died to train a new generation of distinguished conservative
and moderate academics. But after another decade or so of retirements,
deaths, and biased academic hiring, to recruit such a faculty would
become a good deal more difficult, making the decline of American
universities harder to reverse.

We need good universities in the same way that we need reliable
electricity and safe drinking water. We can do without them if we must,

but before long the disadvantages and dangers of doing without them will become more and more evident. Conservativism and moderate liberalism, and moderates and conservatives themselves, will continue to suffer from exclusion from most of the institutions that shape the knowledge and thinking of the majority of the population with some higher education. Both conservatism and conservatives will become either less conservative or (more likely) more anti-intellectual. Universities, professors, and students will continue to be denied exposure to much fundamental knowledge, to a free exchange of ideas, and indeed to any ideas that are incompatible with a leftist ideology deaf to criticism. Both America and the world, which still needs American leadership, will suffer from a worsening ideological schism between increasingly intolerant leftists and increasingly anti-intellectual conservatives. By now, even many professors are distressed by what they have done to American higher education, without having clear ideas of how to repair the damage. Here I shall try to explain that damage in more detail and to suggest how we might start to repair it.

Chapter 2

THE PROBLEMS

The Decline of the University

Have American universities declined beyond hope of recovery? Of course not. They have been in decline only for about fifty years, and in another fifty years they may well improve. Right now, however, the signs are not good. American college degrees have never cost more and never meant less. The majority of high school graduates now enter college, because most well-paid jobs require at least a college degree and often a graduate degree, for which a college degree is a prerequisite. Four years of college will cost new students on average more than $75,000 at public institutions and $150,000 at private institutions—and college takes most students more than four years.[1] Despite having enormous endowments, Harvard, Princeton, Yale, and Stanford will charge new students over $200,000 for four years.[2] Though the real cost to students is often less because of scholarships, it keeps rising by far more than the rate of inflation. Over 44 million borrowers, many of whom never earned a degree, owe more than $1.4 trillion in student loans.[3] Yet colleges offer programs of study that usually consist of a series of mediocre courses on unrelated subjects that fail to provide either a coherent education or adequate training for any job. Nonetheless, most students seem to be content with what they get, apparently because their main interest is in enjoying themselves away from home and avoiding much academic effort, as long as their grades look good on their transcripts. Politicians, university administrators, and professors can always be found to insist that American colleges and universities are the best in the world and that the main problem is that not enough Americans go to college or graduate from it.[4]

The state of the American university remains precarious for several reasons. College costs and student debt have reached a level beyond which they cannot keep rising indefinitely. Colleges keep expanding their use of badly paid adjunct professors hired after only a perfunctory look at their credentials. These adjuncts increased from about 13 percent of the faculty in 1988 to about 51 percent in 2011; in 2011 another 29 percent were instructors not eligible for tenure, and only 21 percent were tenured professors.[5] Meanwhile, a growing number of courses are available on the Internet, many for free, raising the question of why students should pay as much as $4,000 for a classroom course when they can take a better course for much less or for nothing. At the same time, many American voters, state legislators, and governors who have a low opinion of professors and their ideas are becoming still more reluctant to subsidize higher education through taxes. Between 1987 and 2012, state and local spending on higher education per full-time student fell by 30.6 percent in constant dollars, while tuition at state and local institutions rose by 100.5 percent.[6]

Most recent books on American universities have been critical, many devastatingly so. Not even most professors and administrators are truly happy with the present state of universities. Two recent critics observe that American "college and university professors often express surprisingly low levels of job satisfaction."[7] The president of the American Association of University Professors (AAUP) has summed up the consensus among faculty: "The sad truth is that US higher education is in decline."[8] A poll in 2012 showed that 89 percent of American adults and 96 percent of senior academic administrators agree that American higher education is "in crisis."[9] When a recent dean of Harvard College writes a book subtitled *How a Great University Forgot Education* and laments "the loss of purpose in America's great colleges"—meaning Harvard, Yale, Princeton, and the other elite universities that follow their lead—the presumption must be that something has gone very wrong.[10] These are the opinions of academics, most of whom are by no means conservative.

Some authorities still insist that colleges, even if they teach no specific knowledge, at least improve "critical thinking." But this contention is not borne out by a test designed to measure such thinking, the
Collegiate Learning Assessment (CLA). Since the 1980s the improvement
in students' CLA scores during their four years of college has dropped
by about 50 percent, and such improvement now averages just 7 percent
over the first three semesters. Even that small gain is very unevenly
distributed: the top 10 percent of students average a creditable improvement of 43 percent, but about 45 percent of students show no significant
improvement at all.[11] Another test of academic proficiency given by the
Educational Testing Service (ETS) found that between 2006 and 2011
the number of students who were "proficient" in "critical thinking"
rose during four years of college only from 3 percent to 8 percent; those
"proficient" in "written communication" rose only from 5 percent to 9
percent; and those "proficient" in mathematics rose only from 5 percent
to 10 percent. (Presumably the 8–10 percent of proficient graduates
are more or less the same as that top 10 percent who showed strong
improvement in critical thinking according to the CLA.) Leaving aside
a "marginal" category, the number who were clearly "not proficient"
decreased during their college years only from 86 percent to 72 percent in
"critical thinking," only from 77 percent to 63 percent in "written communication," and only from 84 percent to 73 percent in mathematics.[12]
Such measures are hard to dismiss, because if anything the ETS has an
incentive to tell colleges what they want to hear.

One important reason few students learn much at college is probably that they spend so little time studying. A recent survey found that
studying took up an average of only about 7 percent of students' time at
college, and even much of that time was wasted in "studying" along with
other students, which brought no improvement in learning and amount-
ed to not much more than socializing.[13] Another survey found that the
time students spent on homework and classes combined dropped from
about forty hours a week in 1961 to about twenty-seven hours a week
in 2004; homework alone fell by almost half, from about twenty-four
hours a week to just fourteen hours.[14] Most students seemed to regard
college mostly as a chance to have fun before having to work at a job or
go to professional school.[15] While such students certainly deserve much
of the blame for their failure to learn, professors should also be blamed

for their lenient demands and easy grading. The average college student, despite spending so little time studying and learning so little, has a grade point average of 3.2, or a high B−; students at elite colleges, who appear not to study much more than the others, receive still higher grades.[16] Thus nearly half of college students seem to be studying very little and learning very little—surely not enough to be worth anyone's spending $100,000 or more for it.

Costs could of course be cut by having students take their undergraduate degrees in four years instead of five, six, seven, or eight. About twenty-five years ago, some of us who taught at Florida International University (FIU), a large state institution in Miami, noticed that many of our classes had no space for freshmen or sophomores because juniors and seniors, who registered first, were repeating the classes several times. Students who were dissatisfied with their grades (often because they got an F for skipping papers or exams) took the same course over and over again, thanks to university rules that let them replace the first grade on their transcript with the new one. My greatest achievement in the Faculty Senate was passing a rule that students could take the same course only four times. (My original proposal limiting it to three times was considered too radical.) One of my colleagues noted that one problem was that tuition, which the faculty did not control, was too low (then $300 a course, now $638 a course). A worse problem was that many of our students were completely uninterested in their education and cared only about the grades on their transcript.

Admissions officers are also to blame: many of the students they admit to colleges, often chosen using criteria with only the most marginal relevance to academic ability, are not ready to do college-level work. Around 25 percent of those admitted to four-year colleges and around 58 percent of those admitted to two-year colleges require remedial courses, and fewer than half of these students pass all the remedial courses they need; even a large number of those who manage to pass the remedial courses fail to graduate later.[17] Whether because of a lack of ability, lack of preparation, lack of effort, or a combination of all three, students' college completion rates are poor. Almost a third of the students who enroll in (supposedly) four-year colleges fail to graduate within eight and a half years, and almost two-thirds of those who enroll in (supposedly) two-year colleges fail to graduate within six years. At for-profit "four-year" colleges, the six-year graduation rate is a mere 22 percent.[18] Consequently many students either graduate after taking far too long, at a greatly increased cost and often with a large debt, or never graduate at all, with no degree to show for a large investment and often a large debt. Those who fail to graduate represent a waste of resources by almost any measure.

While the amount of money spent on American education is obviously too high, concentrating on cutting costs seems questionable when the product is of such minimal value for so many students. For instance, what is the point of having professors teach a larger number of courses from which students learn little or nothing? Even if the average price for a public college education could be cut by a third, $50,000 is still far too much to pay for students not to learn anything. If all students want is to enjoy themselves on a break from studying and working, and the rest of us for some reason consider this desirable, they should be able to enjoy themselves for much less money, perhaps for a year at a pleasant place where they can live in comfortable dormitories and party, sunbathe, or ski with no classes to feel guilty about skipping. If the quality of a college education cannot be improved, we should concentrate on encouraging at least half of those who now go to college not to go, adjusting requirements for jobs and professional schools accordingly, and making provisions for an orderly shutdown or shrinking of most of our colleges and universities. But of course the quality of a college education *can* be improved. The problem is that hardly anyone is trying to improve it. Few people are even paying attention to the defects of higher education as it is now, and some still deny that anything is wrong.

Sources of the Problems

Although most students start with little knowledge of the subjects they study, introductory courses have become hard to find, and even some courses that look introductory give very limited impressions of their subjects. In the words of Louis Menand, who taught at Princeton and the City University of New York before becoming a professor at Harvard, after 1970 "courses became much more specialized; that is, the broad survey or introductory course began to disappear, something that is usually a symptom of uncertainty about the essential character of a discipline."[19] Instead students have "distribution requirements" that are satisfied by whatever specialized courses interest the professors who teach them. As the disillusioned former Harvard dean mentioned earlier says of Harvard's misnamed "Core Curriculum," "Students eager to understand the world in which they were living were puzzled, for example, that the Core course *Gendered Communities: Women, Islam, and Nationalism in the Middle East and North Africa* satisfied a requirement but the History Department course *The World in the Twentieth Century* did not."[20] A prominent graduate notes that while he was at Harvard (1998–2002) it never offered a course on the American Revolution.[21] In most colleges the majority of students graduate without having read anything by Homer, Sophocles, Plato, Shakespeare, Milton, or Dickens. Students may even have been taught to be proud of not having read those "elitist dead white males." Most students never learn that even the illiterate listened to Homer's poems and the plays of Sophocles and Shakespeare, or that even people with only an elementary education bought the novels of Dickens and Thackeray in cheap paperbound parts. Though you do need a good education to appreciate Plato or Milton, a good education should be what you go to college to get.

In most colleges students are also supposed to receive a "multicultural" education that will familiarize them with the different cultures of the world. In principle, learning about different cultures is an unexceptionable idea. But in practice it usually means learning about a fictional world imagined by American leftists: a feminist Africa, a pacifist Islam, Hinduism without the caste system, Roman pagans who never persecuted Christians, Aztecs who never practiced human sacrifice, a benevolent Soviet Union and Maoist China, and a malevolent United States and Western Europe. In the words of a professor at Dartmouth, "In fact, multiculturalism is an ideological fantasy maintained in obvious bad faith. It really amounts to a form of anti-Westernism."[22] Students are often told that history and other academic disciplines, including the natural sciences, are composed of "myths" created as a means of oppression by the powerful, giving students one more excuse for not studying.[23]

A generally sympathetic history of Harvard published in 2001 found that "a new, postmodern skepticism with regard to objectivity and truth" and "political correctness, with its deadening effect on the free exchange of ideas," are "less evident at Harvard than at many other universities," but nevertheless "it is arguable that Harvard today is no more open to diversity of thought than it was at the height of the cold war during the 1950s."[24] (The authors cannot quite bring themselves to make their comparison to McCarthyism explicit.) Harvard's former president Derek Bok admits that "it does seem clear beyond dispute that faculty members whose political orientation inclines to the liberal side far outnumber those whose views lie to the right or the conservative side."[25] Louis Menand again sums up the situation: "Professors tend increasingly to think alike because the profession is increasingly self-selected. The university may not explicitly require conformity on more than scholarly matters, but the existing system implicitly demands and constructs it."[26]

"Postmodernism," a term that will recur in the pages that follow, stands for something too amorphous to be easily defined, but the literary theorist Terry Eagleton provides a definition that is better than most:

> By "postmodern," I mean, roughly speaking, the contemporary movement of thought which rejects totalities, universal values, grand historical narratives, solid foundations to human existence and the possibility of objective knowledge. Postmodernism is skeptical of truth, unity and progress, opposes what it sees as elitism in culture, tends towards cultural relativism, and celebrates pluralism, discontinuity and heterogeneity.[27]

Postmodernism is almost impossible to combat on its own terms, because rejecting the possibility of objective truth allows postmodernists to ignore even the most rigorous arguments and conclusive evidence, and their rejection of "elitism" often leads them to deny that any idea is better than any other. Despite denying any possible validity of their opponents' ideas and arguments, they insist that their own ideas are preferable because they are anti-elitist.

Marxists, feminists, and other ideologues often ally themselves with postmodernists because all of them judge arguments not on their objective merits but on ideological grounds. Such an attitude can easily lead to an ideological attack on any academic standards and a general celebration of mediocrity—as long as the mediocrity is of the required leftist kind. Leftist mediocrity naturally has a strong appeal for mediocre leftist professors, even for those who know little about postmodernist,

Marxist, feminist, or other theories. Postmodernism may have less appeal for students, of whom only about 7 percent now major in the humanities. At Harvard, the number of humanities majors declined by 20 percent between 2003 and 2013, because "most students who say they intend to major in the humanities end up in other fields"—in other words, they give up on the humanities after they see how Harvard teaches the humanities.[28] Many had probably thought humanities majors at Harvard would deal with great literature or historical facts, and chose other majors once they discovered they were wrong.

A large part of the problem is that for various reasons many professors are teaching badly. One expert recently concluded that an increased emphasis on teaching since the 1980s has actually made teaching *less effective*, because "progressive education practices align well with the priorities of student culture, which has been interested in enjoyable activities, but not as interested in demanding requirements and high standards that would help to increase skill development and learning." This "has helped to diminish the status and perhaps also the net social contribution of the [academic] profession."[29] Emphasizing teaching—without improving it—has incidentally encouraged professors to do less serious research, so that according to the same expert, "after decades of U.S. dominance, in recent years European scholars have taken over the lead in scientific publication."[30] Seemingly the easiest way to satisfy almost everyone, including critics who think professors should do more teaching, would be to have each professor offer fifty courses or so, never see students or assign any work, and give everyone an A. Yet soon everyone would realize that this solution made the faculty superfluous. The growing prevalence of adjunct professors indicates that regular professors are already becoming unnecessary.

The current system of faculty training, hiring, and governance, even if it were sustainable, is bizarre and dysfunctional. Graduate schools now produce far more new doctorates than the academic positions available for them, and most of these new doctorates are poorly trained for any positions that are not academic. The problem is serious in the humanities and social sciences but not limited to them: even in science and engineering, doctorates outnumber available jobs by about three to one.[31] Moreover, the academic job market is likely to grow worse in coming years. Student enrollments are already starting to fall as rising costs deter more potential students from going to college.[32] More adjunct professors are being hired to replace the regular faculty who retire. Meanwhile, the last of the regular faculty hired during the academic boom that ended in 1970 are retiring, leaving only the much smaller numbers who were first hired during the seventies and eighties as the next cohort to retire. Finally, online courses, even if they turn out to have less impact on higher education than many people now expect, are almost certain to reduce the number of professors to some extent.

Despite poor prospects for employment, the number of graduate students in the pipeline seems not to be decreasing significantly. Most of these graduate students are not even well trained as academics. Graduate courses, like undergraduate courses, consist of whatever the professors want to teach and are often highly specialized and poorly suited to the graduate students' needs and interests. Grading for graduate students is even easier than for undergraduates; the vast majority of graduate students' grades are As. Most graduate students take at least one general qualifying examination, but they seldom fail it, and when they do fail they can retake it and usually pass the second time. Then they write a doctoral dissertation, generally on a specialized subject from a narrow point of view. They often receive little help from their professors, but almost any dissertation is accepted. Usually everyone assumes it will take years to be made acceptable for publication. This assumption is actually built into the system, because even the few PhDs who get a job right away are allowed six years before they come up for tenure, which is the first time they are likely to need to have published a book. Once again, Louis Menand says what almost all professors know but seldom say: "The idea that the doctoral thesis is a rigorous requirement is belied by the quality of most doctoral theses."[33]

Advertisements for tenure-track faculty positions often attract one to two hundred applicants. Even a hundred application files can be overwhelming for the small search committee of regular faculty that must screen them. The professors serving on search committees seldom have any specialized knowledge of the subject for which they are hiring; after all, the point of the search is to hire a specialist in a field not currently represented in the department, and even if the new hire is replacing a departing professor, that professor is seldom consulted, on the theory that the old professor will "not need to live with" the new hire. Along with transcripts of grades, nearly all As, the applicants' files consist of letters of recommendation that are nearly all glowing, because the professors who wrote them want their students to get jobs. The search committee can request writing samples but scarcely ever has time to read them if it does; just skimming all those files is very time-consuming. Only a few candidates can be eliminated at a glance as clearly unqualified. The number of candidates can however be reduced by putting artificially specialized criteria in the advertisement and then eliminating all applicants without those qualifications. Sometimes the ad is made so specific that it fits only one candidate, whom members of the department know personally and want to hire without bothering to consider anyone else.

The pool of candidates can be reduced further by considering only female or minority candidates or candidates with fashionable approaches, who can quickly be identified by skimming the files. Many will already have published articles or book chapters, usually based on their dissertations, before or after receiving their doctorates. Since having "too many publications" before getting a tenure-track job is taken to mean that the candidate is "overqualified," or at any rate has failed to impress previous search committees, a few fashionable publications are best. Editorial committees as well as hiring committees are likely to find fashionable but fallacious work more interesting than solid and careful work, which non-specialists may consider boring. A candidate with something important to say about his specialty will not necessarily appeal to committee members with other specialties; but a candidate with something postmodern to say about his specialty will appeal to all the postmodernists in the department, as well as others who want to keep up with such "innovative" work. Since committees pay so little attention to each file, one popular tactic in articles, dissertations, and letters of application is to refer on the first page or so to a postmodernist, particularly Michel Foucault. An analogous situation seems to occur in the natural sciences, where journals and hiring committees prefer researchers who reach striking results with little attention to accuracy. The *Economist* recently noted in a cover article that many scientific articles are "a load of rubbish," because "cut-throat" competition for jobs leads applicants to "the cherry-picking of results" and "spurious correlations" so as to have their work accepted by "journals eager for startling papers."[34]

There are other informal rules for hiring. For example, having taught at a community college or secondary school after receiving one's doctorate is an almost insuperable obstacle, though having taught as an adjunct professor at a four-year institution is not. The reason seems to be that professors at four-year colleges want to think that all such places are incomparably superior to community colleges and even the best secondary schools, though even on that dubious assumption one might doubt that having taught at an inferior institution should disqualify an otherwise excellent candidate. For the most prestigious universities, having a tenure-track job at an obscure college is nearly as disqualifying. Another almost fatal defect for many hiring committees is having been denied tenure, except at a handful of elite universities like Harvard, Princeton, Yale, or Stanford, which often deny tenure to candidates who would have received it elsewhere. For the same reason, anything even slightly negative in a letter of recommendation is usually disqualifying: a negative comment or denial of tenure is assumed, sometimes correctly, to conceal a serious weakness or even a scandal. Rumors that someone is a troublemaker are also a very serious drawback. Yet obnoxious people can do quite well in academia—if they are smart enough to behave themselves during interviews and wait to annoy their colleagues until after being hired or given tenure.

Using such procedures, search committee members typically settle on a short list of ten to twelve applicants to interview at the annual convention for their discipline, or by phone or Skype. This short list is then winnowed to one to three finalists, who are interviewed on campus by the whole department. On campus the finalist gives a presentation, which may be a scholarly lecture, an informal discussion, or an undergraduate class. The decisive criterion in both sets of interviews tends to be "collegiality"—that is, how well the candidates "fit into the department," which often means little more than how well the interviewers like them personally. In departments that are split into factions, of which there are many, another major factor is how each candidate could be expected to vote in future departmental meetings. Reasons given for eliminating excellent candidates include "She wouldn't come to a place like this anyway," "He wouldn't fit in here," "She wouldn't be happy here," or "We're primarily a teaching department, and his main interest is obviously research." On such grounds many of the finest academics of earlier generations, from Albert Einstein to Vladimir Nabokov, would be eliminated at the interview stage today.[35] Though the relevant college administrators must approve the final selection, they almost always do so. The whole process includes a large element of chance and very seldom results in hiring the best scholar or the best teacher. In fact, few professors or administrators involved in this process anywhere try to hire the best possible candidate.

Once hired, the new assistant professor has a probationary period before coming up for tenure in his sixth year, and a seventh, terminal year if tenure is denied. Except at a very few elite institutions, tenure is usually granted. Many departments, especially those that say they mainly value teaching, do not require a published book, and though they usually require at least one published article, their assistant professors can submit articles to many journals, including some that are not at all selective. Assistant professors are also expected to deliver conference papers, but many conferences accept almost all submissions. Some conference papers are collected in published books, often with less attention to quality than articles submitted to journals. For assistant professors at institutions that require books, some presses are minimally selective. The more fashionable the subject, the more likely the press is to accept the book, because such books sell better. One can submit a revised dissertation for publication again and again, each time taking into account the comments from the last rejection.[36] As for teaching, most teaching evaluations are favorable, and anyone can practically ensure good evaluations by requiring little to no reading or writing, then giving every student an A.[37] Thus, if you are lucky enough to get a tenure-track job, you will probably get tenure, and the exceptions are most often the few who have somehow offended their colleagues or administrators.

In many cases, excellence can hurt an aspiring academic. Although search committee members have reason to reject candidates so obviously incompetent as to discredit their departments, a department composed of people who have published only an article or two will be very reluctant to hire someone likely to publish a book, let alone someone who has already had one accepted. How will that make the rest of them look when it comes time for annual evaluations? Why, the new hire could end up with nearly all the money for merit raises in the whole department! Even a department with senior professors who have all published books can be leery of applicants who look as if they may publish more, and the current star of the department may not want to share the firmament with a rising star. Besides, what if a department hires someone whom its members later turn out not to like personally? If he publishes widely and clearly performs well, they could have all sorts of trouble denying him tenure. Much the safest and easiest course is to hire someone who looks all right but is actually not very good and who can be denied tenure if necessary.

If a department chooses a candidate who does fashionable research or is a woman or a member of a minority, it can readily explain why it failed to hire more-qualified candidates: the department needs to have people who do work "on the cutting edge" or needs to increase its "diversity." If some female, minority, or fashionable candidates are too good, another female, minority, or fashionable candidate who is less threatening can be hired while still adhering to the principles of "the cutting edge" or "diversity." An institution can always find some reason to prefer an undistinguished candidate by invoking the department's need either to fill its supposed gaps or to build on its supposed strengths. ("We have nobody who does early Joyce!" "If we hire just one more Joyce specialist, we'll have the most of any English department in the Midwest!") Often no one will ask for a reason for even the most outrageous hires, much less a logical reason. The great majority of hires are made at the entry level not because junior hires are cheaper—over the length of the scholars' careers they cost much more than senior hires—but because departments are reluctant to hire professors with proven records of achievement, who can make their colleagues look bad right away and cannot be denied tenure because they have already received it.

These various syndromes explain why the enormous oversupply of candidates has led to little if any improvement in the quality of professors, as one might otherwise expect. During almost fifty years of a desperately bad job market for applicants, when even mediocre departments could have made consistently outstanding hires, the relative academic reputations of top universities and departments have barely budged, and the few changes have resulted more often from the decline of some departments than from the advance of others. Very rarely, one or two determined professors have exploited the situation to create an excellent department at a mediocre university, like the Department of Philosophy at Auburn University in Alabama; but this is unusual enough to warrant an article in the *New York Times Magazine*.[38] Nor has any other university tried to hire away the excellent professors of the Auburn philosophy department, as many universities could easily have done. A sustained effort to make consistently outstanding hires could surely have allowed, say, Stanford or Columbia to gain an academic reputation as the best university in the country ahead of Harvard and Princeton, or Emory or Rice to overtake the reputation of Stanford or Columbia. Even universities far down the academic totem pole could have come to be ranked among the country's finest. Yet no such thing has happened. Since professors tend to hire other professors no better and not much worse than themselves, institutional reputations remain more or less stable.

Though reputations are subjective by definition, there is a remarkable degree of consensus about university reputations, which in my experience is roughly correct. The annual rankings of best colleges by *U.S. News and World Report* depend heavily on a "peer assessment score," meaning an opinion poll of other academics, which is simply a measure of institutional reputation. The overall rankings are weighted unfairly in favor of private institutions, which tend to have the smaller class sizes and higher graduation, student retention, and alumni giving rates that *U.S. News* values. Such factors do however reflect a general tendency for private institutions to pay more attention to their students than public ones do. The *U.S. News* ratings can also be manipulated to some degree. For example, colleges can arrange to have a higher percentage of classes with fewer than twenty students, which *U.S. News* likes, by putting some students in many small classes and most students in a few enormous classes. Yet even this practice allows good students to choose small classes and mediocre students to choose the giant ones, which tend to be less rigorous and offer protection from the dreaded fate of being called on by a professor. While naturally at every university some departments are better than others, the administration and the institutional culture tend to drag down good departments at mediocre universities, though they improve the reputations of weaker departments at better universities more often than they actually improve the departments.

The failure of American universities to improve is no more the fault of professors than of university administrators, who could have insisted on hiring better professors but have not. Most administrators have poor academic qualifications themselves and tend to prefer mediocre faculty, who can be paid less and are less likely than distinguished faculty to complain about their salaries or to question administrative decisions. The administrators at Auburn University were so unhappy with their exceptionally good philosophy department that they first tried to manipulate the criteria that demonstrated the department's excellence and finally decided to ignore the criteria entirely.[39] And if you want to find a single group to blame for the steadily rising cost of an American college education, administrators are much more plausible villains than professors. Since 1970 full-time professors have been receiving raises that have barely kept up with inflation, and average professorial salaries have dropped catastrophically if the averages include adjunct professors.[40] But administrative costs have soared as more and more administrators have been paid better and better. Between 1975 and 2005 the number of college and university administrators and their staff grew from about 60 percent of the number of full-time faculty to about 112 percent.[41] Administrators are also responsible for a vast amount of wasteful spending and useless or even harmful programs.[42]

At Harvard, some 40 percent of the 2007 budget went for administration and only some 29 percent for instruction, with some 18 percent for "research and service" and 13 percent for "other." Although Harvard's administration is unusually large and expensive, the percentage of its budget spent on instruction is very much in line with other institutions. The national averages are about 29.5 percent for instruction, 19 percent for administration, 25 percent for "research and service," and 26 percent for "other."[43] Administrators are chiefly responsible for making "other" a large item in universities' budgets, including grandiose buildings that are costly to maintain, elaborate student centers, beer pubs, climbing walls, and lavish intercollegiate sports programs, most of which do very little for education and sometimes detract from it.[44] Even university computer labs are often used by students more to play computer games than for academic purposes.[45] No doubt universities need some administrators and buildings, and faculty research can benefit not only education but society at large. Nevertheless, the overall cost of American "education" could probably be cut by about a third by slashing administration, construction, and sports without doing any harm to real education.

Problematic Solutions

The best-informed critics realize that most students are happy to take long and expensive vacations at college and to receive high grades and a degree at the end, while most professors are willing to give their students high grades after spending very little time on correcting papers or examinations, and most administrators are pleased to be well paid for presiding over contented students and hiring discontented adjunct professors at low pay. Current trends seem to be leading to colleges with more expensive buildings and administrations, where students receive excellent grades for having fun and where courses and professors are of poor quality but unimportant. Having recently read or skimmed dozens of books on American higher education, I notice that since the 1990s they have become less frequent, while the tone of the more recent books has become more desperate. One of the more recent books observes that "many commentators cannot suppress the fear that what is happening in the realm of higher education in the United States is absolutely terrifying."[46] Scarcely anyone says that the situation is getting better, but the sort of people who write books about it have apparently begun to despair that anything can be done. Although identifying a problem is the first stage in solving it, this problem has been identified for a long time without coming any closer to a solution.

Most proposed solutions have been extremely vague. For example, the disillusioned Harvard dean Harry Lewis declares in his mostly admirable book, "We must find a way to honor good character in our faculty and to penalize acts that call a professor's character into question." Then he admits, "The evaluation of character is easier said than done," and never tells us how to do it.[47] Another recent book, memorably titled *We're Losing Our Minds: Rethinking American Higher Education*, ends with a chapter entitled "Talk of Change Is Not Change," which comes to this conclusion: "Cultural problems require cultural solutions, starting with a national conversation about what is wrong, and what is needed, in higher education."[48] This sounds much less like change than like talk about change, especially because the authors make no clear suggestions about how to conduct such a "national conversation." The most detailed study of the ineffectiveness of American colleges, entitled *Academically Adrift*, calls for "instilling in the next generation of young adults a lifelong love of learning, an ability to think critically and communicate effectively, and a willingness to embrace and assume adult responsibilities," again without explaining how this ambitious and laudable program could be implemented.[49]

Harvard's former president Bok asks an excellent question in his recent and lengthy volume on American higher education:

> What was it about Athens in the fifth century BC, or Florence in the fifteenth century AD, or, for that matter, Budapest around the turn of the twentieth century that produced so many people of such exceptional creativity and talent? If [university] presidents could only understand that, they might be able to bring about something really remarkable in their own university.[50]

Just fifty pages later, however, Bok comes to this conclusion: "In the end, the key ingredients of progress will be a determination on the part of academic leaders to concentrate on raising graduation rates *and* improving the quality of education coupled with a willingness on the part of public officials, foundations, and other donors to support the research and experimentation required before embarking on expensive reforms of unproven value."[51] In other words, the same people who have created our problems in higher education, which Bok admits are serious, need to commission a series of further studies (on top of the great many cited by Bok) before deciding whether anything whatever should be done. Athens, Florence, and Budapest are forgotten.

A few observers do make clear suggestions—the abolition of tenure is a perennial favorite—but without demonstrating how such changes would help.[52] For instance, the Obama administration had the idea of basing federal aid on a ranking of colleges by tuition, student debt, graduation rates, and graduate earnings, though once this information was made available, the plan to base federal funding on it was abandoned after severe criticism.[53] The plan included no efforts to improve the quality of instruction, and in practice the criteria would often undermine each other. College administrators can easily reduce tuition and student debt by hiring more adjunct faculty without regard for quality and by admitting higher-income students who can pay full tuition without scholarships or loans. Graduation rates can be increased most easily by more grade inflation, beer pubs, and climbing walls for the "students" with no interest in studying, who would leave without such enticements. The easiest way to increase the earnings of graduates is to admit higher-income students in the first place, then encourage them to go into high-paying professions and to avoid teaching or charitable work (the reverse of what the Obama administration otherwise seemed to want). Conversely, attracting lower-income students can be done most easily by lowering academic standards further. Right now, the institutions that seem to be best at attracting low-income students are low-quality, for-profit schools that offer vocational credentials of dubious value. Such vocational schools are a real problem, but they are not typical of the rest of American higher education and can best be reformed by a better system of accreditation.[54]

Bernie Sanders, followed by Hillary Clinton against her better judgment, has proposed that tuition be free at public colleges and universities for almost all students in their home states. This proposal is sure to be expensive, because—to begin with—the federal and state governments would need to replace all the money now collected from tuition at public institutions. Then, unless enrollments were strictly capped, the proposal would become still more expensive, because free tuition would lure many students away from public institutions in other states, where they now pay higher tuition, and from private institutions, which now cost governments nothing in tuition. Many of the less prestigious private institutions would surely go bankrupt, causing the usual job losses and economic problems that go with bankruptcies. Free tuition would also attract many young and older people who are now not in college and currently cost the government nothing. Unless public higher education expanded enormously, it would need to become much more selective, excluding many students who now qualify for it. If public education did expand, it would cost still more money. In any case, "free tuition" would greatly increase public spending, much of which would go to students who would probably take more time and study even less than current students, now that they had no debts, work-study jobs, or nagging parents to worry about. (In other countries with free public higher education and easy admissions, most students do little studying, stay enrolled for many years, and earn degrees of little value, if they graduate at all.) Why taxpayers without children in public colleges and universities should pay for all this is unclear.

Recently the suggestion has been made that colleges and universities should be required to give their graduating students exit examinations and make the results public to show what the graduates have learned.[55] Although this suggestion is fine in theory, in practice it would probably not make enough difference to justify the trouble of implementing it. Setting and grading a good examination would be hard, because few people have a clear idea of what universities should do, least of all the institutions themselves; the universities would likely advocate a postmodern "inclusive" and "multicultural" exit examination that would make matters worse. If the examination were a good one, most graduates would do badly, including most graduates of elite universities; but the educational establishment would use these results to attack the examination and argue for a different one or no exam at all. No doubt the graduates of elite universities would do better than other graduates, simply because they came from better-educated families and had gone to better primary and secondary schools. In any case, the results would give few institutions much incentive to improve. Universities have had no trouble ignoring the results of the similar Collegiate Learning Assessment, mentioned above.[56]

So students, professors, parents, and the rest of us are left pretty much on our own. Students applying to college are the most directly affected but are also the ones least equipped to decide what to do. If you are a student, in principle you should attend the best college you can and choose your courses there very carefully. In practice, this is not so easy. Even many of the best colleges have a curriculum that will force you to take some very inferior courses and make it hard for you to tell how good your courses are before you take them. You will also need to figure out for yourself what a good education is today, a matter on which most authorities disagree, if they have even thought about it. You and your parents can spend a great deal of time reading and researching colleges in the abstract and in particular and emerge even more confused than you were in the first place. My own research on universities has left me not at all certain what to advise students who are thinking of applying to college.

Reliable advice on colleges is hard to find. For example, William

Bennett, secretary of education under President Reagan and a brilliant conservative critic of American universities, recommends, among other places, Hillsdale College.[57] Hillsdale once fired me after I protested its administration's harassment of student and faculty critics, especially a defamation lawsuit against a professor that was dropped after he was made to pay ruinous legal fees. (The real purpose was to cover up the alcoholic president's arrest for drunken driving.) The AAUP investigated the case and censured Hillsdale for violating my academic freedom.[58] The dean who fired me later apologized to me after he was demoted himself. Of the six institutions where I have taught (with regular appointments at Hillsdale, Florida International University, and Saint Louis University, and visiting appointments at UCLA, Stanford, and Berkeley), Hillsdale was the worst, with a hopelessly muddled curriculum and a mostly lack-luster faculty that the president himself ridiculed in private. Even after that president was forced to resign because of a sex scandal, Hillsdale has never responded to the AAUP's annual inquiries about my case. Though I left Hillsdale in 1988, while I was there it was being praised by conservative commentators in almost exactly the same terms as it is now. I am similarly skeptical about sweeping claims made for various other small liberal arts colleges that sound a lot like Hillsdale.

If you are a professor, you should teach and write as well as you can. You should volunteer to serve on faculty search committees, which are unpopular assignments because they involve so much work. You can also serve on the faculty senate or faculty council, to which you can probably be elected because most professors also find them too much work. Some of your students will appreciate your teaching, but others will complain that you assign too much reading and writing and are too hard a grader. You may feel a certain satisfaction in the way you teach your own classes, but you will still know that those classes are a small part of what will be a poor education for most of your students. Your efforts will win you few friends among your colleagues, because your good teaching and research will make others' teaching and research look worse. Your initiatives in the faculty senate or council will be unpopular if they are contrary to the interests of other faculty members or administrators, as the most use-ful initiatives probably will be. Your efforts to hire good new professors will meet with opposition from your colleagues, who will accuse you of racism and sexism unless all your candidates are minorities or women.

Even if you succeed in hiring one or two good new professors, they will think (correctly) that they deserved to be hired on their merits, and they may well be unhappy that they were not hired at a better institution, may think that trying to make their new department better is not worth the time, effort, and aggravation, and may see no reason to hire another good professor who might make them look less exceptional. My experience over forty years has been that one professor can do very little alone.

Could a group of professors do more? That possibility has been explored by the National Association of Scholars, founded in 1987. It describes itself as "working to foster intellectual freedom and to sustain the tradition of reasoned scholarship and civil debate in America's colleges and universities" and advocating "excellence by encouraging commitment to high intellectual standards, individual merit, institutional integrity, good governance, and sound public policy."[59] These are estimable goals, and I myself have been a member almost from the start. The NAS has done some real good by calling attention to the sorts of problems mentioned here. Yet I regret to say that it has failed in most of its aims. It has attracted a small group of excellent professors who are worried about leftist bias in higher education and are ready to defend excellence publicly, along with a larger group of less excellent professors who are also worried about leftist bias. To use contemporary jargon, the NAS has served as a support group for an oppressed minority who are victims of pervasive discrimination and a hostile work environment. But professors and graduate students who join the NAS run the real risk of harming their careers and can expect few benefits. While the NAS has defended some people who needed defending and often made and sometimes enacted good proposals, its worthy efforts have made little progress toward solving the enormous problems it has identified.[60] Heterodox Academy, a newer group that includes liberals and some leftists, so far has mainly publicized issues of diversity of opinion in universities without offering plans for concrete action.[61]

What can we do as voters, parents, alumni, and citizens? Many people think that we should just let the system collapse under its own weight, helping it along by voting for legislators who cut expenditures for higher education and try to abolish tenure. Most Americans have nothing like tenure and think they work harder than tenured professors, most of whom spend just five to ten hours a week in the classroom and perhaps as much again on course preparation and grading. (The fact that I have written ten books and sixty-odd articles and book chapters while serving on many search committees shows that my own teaching duties left me plenty of time.) After all, colleges could save a lot of money by having all their remaining tenured professors replaced by adjuncts (who typically receive between $2,000 and $6,000 per course and no benefits, often less than the tuition paid for the course by a single student). On the other hand, most of us would be troubled by the prospect of having the next generation, including our own children, taught all their courses by impoverished and embittered adjuncts hired almost at random. Treated badly and given no hope of anything better, most of the best adjuncts will likely leave teaching, as they eventually do now. With not even a remote prospect of tenure or a decent salary in the future, many fewer good students will go on to graduate school, and the pool of adjuncts will shrink and further decline in quality. Such a collapse of higher education—including the economic ruin of hundreds of thousands of formerly tenured professors—would surely be bad for America.

A growing number of Americans are losing faith in higher education altogether. When asked in a poll in 2012, "Do you think young people today need a four-year college degree to be successful?" 61 percent of Americans agreed and 37 percent did not; but just a year later, in 2013, only 52 percent agreed and 46 percent did not. In political terms, Republicans disagreed that a college degree was necessary for success by 55 percent to 40 percent, independents disagreed by 50 percent to 48 percent, and only Democrats agreed, by 64 percent to 35 percent.[62] By 2017, a poll showed that only 49 percent of Americans thought college was worth the money and 47 percent thought it was not—a statistical tie.[63] As a general rule, the skeptics happen to be wrong about the advantages of higher education; but they are right if they think this advantage has been decreasing. In 2008, having a college degree instead of just a high school diploma increased the median earnings of graduates aged 25 to 34 by 74 percent for men and 79 percent for women; by 2011 those advantages had dropped to 69 percent for men and 70 percent for women.[64] Obviously some college degrees are much more valuable than others. A study that, according to the *Economist*, "surely overstates the financial value of a college education" reckons the annual return on tuition in increased earnings at between 17.6 percent and *negative* 10.6

percent depending on the institution.[65] As the poor quality of most college instruction becomes better known, the tendencies for more people to think college is less valuable and for college actually to be less valuable are likely to reinforce each other.

In this book I make several specific proposals that I believe would improve American colleges and universities. None of my proposals requires a change in human nature or upending society or the economy. If all or even some of my suggestions were to be adopted, I believe they would decrease the problems of American higher education substantially—though not, of course, eliminate them entirely, as seldom happens with major problems in the real world. Some of the proposals made here would involve legislation, all of it extremely inexpensive by the standards of today's federal budgets and none of it harmful or particularly objectionable to any large segment of the electorate. Whether such legislation is feasible is a matter of public opinion and the political climate, which can be shaped and changed and can sometimes change suddenly, dramatically, and unpredictably. Another proposal suggested here, which requires no legislation, is for a new private university that would be within the means of a number of wealthy donors, all of whom should care about the future of American education and public policy. Whether they would think that a new university is worth funding— rather than, say, giving Harvard more money to spend on ugly buildings or administrative vice presidents—is another question, but a question worth asking.

Chapter 3

THE ORIGINS OF CAMPUS LEFTISM

A Vague but Powerful Ideology

What exactly is the ideology that dominates American campuses today and is increasingly influential off campus? It clearly is intolerant of dissent, but what it actually affirms is so unclear that administrators, faculty, students, and outside speakers are often taken by surprise when their seemingly reasonable remarks or actions provoke frantic protests. Although our universities produce many books and articles influenced by this reigning ideology, few if any of them explain what it actually is. Unlike classical Marxism, the ideas prevalent at today's universities have seldom been the subject of detailed and systematic arguments in books or articles and have generally not spread by means of books or articles.[1] For the most part, leftist faculty and students have made this ideology up as they went along. In educational institutions supposedly dedicated to examining ideas, these ideas have prevailed without being examined. While they constantly develop and change, the changes and additions are seldom explained either. The ideology even lacks a generally accepted name, since "political correctness" is a label for what the dogma demands, not a description of the dogma itself, while "progressivism," "socialism," "inclusivity," "diversity," and "leftism" are vague and overlapping terms used by different people in different contexts.

"Progressivism," perhaps the term campus leftists like best, is not very helpful for defining the ideology's intellectual content. Nearly all of us favor what we consider progress, but many of us disagree about what developments deserve the name of progress. Genetically modified organisms, hydraulic fracturing, and the Keystone XL pipeline look like cases of technological progress to most of us, but most "progressives" oppose them. Many "progressives" are hostile to a wide range of new technologies, on the grounds that they might damage the environment, increase inequality, or oppress minorities. Most "progressives," though insisting on catastrophic predictions of global warming, also insist that the only remedies for it are conservation measures and solar and wind power, which seem inadequate to solve such an enormous problem. Yet the same people oppose large-scale solutions that involve advanced technology, like nuclear power and climate engineering. Many "progressives" oppose objective research not just into climate change but also into many social problems, like whether children do better when raised by both biological parents, black poverty has causes apart from racism, or sexual preferences can be chosen or changed.

"Socialism," a term favored by Bernie Sanders and some of his many student and faculty followers, also fails to capture much of what this ideology is about.[2] The students and professors who admire Sanders scarcely ever advocate state ownership of industry or agriculture; most of them scarcely know or care about factory workers or farmers. Small banks may or may not be better than large banks, but breaking up large private banks into smaller private banks, as Sanders advocates, is not itself a socialist measure. Even "Medicare for all" would leave the provision of medicine to private physicians and hospitals, not to a state health service. Nor is the trade protectionism advocated by Sanders and his partisans particularly socialist—or even progressive. Their proposals to make college tuition or contraceptives free would increase government spending but not government ownership, and they tell us more about the financial concerns of today's college students than about their enthusiasm for statism. Most of today's "socialists" want not more state ownership but more state regulation, except of course for abortion, sexual behavior, and drugs, issues on which they are not socialists but libertarians.

"Inclusivity" and "diversity" are favorite terms on campus, but they call for a striking amount of exclusion and uniformity. "Inclusivity" excludes several large groups like political conservatives, orthodox

Catholics, Evangelical Christians, and Orthodox Jews, since many views held by these groups are considered bigoted and ignorant. Whites, men, and heterosexuals are often attacked as groups and reminded of their "privileged" status and resulting inability to understand others. "Inclusivity" only applies to supposedly oppressed groups like blacks, women, Hispanics, homosexuals, bisexuals, and transsexuals. Their defenders encourage them to engage in identity politics, but in order to emphasize their oppression, not their achievements. "Tolerance" means avoiding not just criticism of these groups but any speech or behavior that could possibly offend them or their defenders. Yet the words and actions that they supposedly find offensive often change and are disputed by the groups themselves. While any criticism of the favored groups is forbidden, even farfetched criticisms of whites, men, and heterosexuals are encouraged. So are accusations of "racism," "sexism," or "homophobia" that are plainly meant to be offensive to the disfavored groups.

One of the main arguments for "diversity" in education used to be that it exposed students to groups other than their own, leading everyone to become more tolerant. Recently, however, the dominant doctrine has become that oppressive groups like whites, men, and heterosexuals cannot possibly understand the oppression endured by the oppressed groups; oppressive groups must accept without question that those other groups are oppressed and that anything they claim oppresses them does so merely because they say it does. If this is so, however, putting whites, men, and heterosexuals on the same campuses with blacks, other races, women, and homosexuals seems likely to bring less tolerance rather than more. Each group will simply learn that it cannot understand the other groups, that the other groups cannot understand it, that attempts by the oppressors to understand the oppressed are themselves oppressive, and that the oppressed have nothing to learn from the oppressors. For example, if all whites are racist by definition, an assumption often made implicitly and sometimes made explicit, for them to try to overcome their racism would appear to be futile. The logical conclusion would seem to be that the oppressed groups should have their own colleges and universities, or at least their own residences and undergraduate majors, as they increasingly do, abandoning "inclusivity" and "diversity." Of course "diversity" has nothing to do with a diversity of opinions, since it refuses to tolerate any dissent from "diversity" as the ideology sees it.

The most neutral and accurate term for this ideology is probably simply "leftism," a term that implies a general attitude rather than a clearly formulated doctrine supported by arguments. The absence of reasoned argument is in fact one of campus leftism's sources of strength. Refusing to supply ideological definitions leaves the impression of a viewpoint that depends not on arguments (which could theoretically be refuted) but is instead so obvious to every decent person that it needs no support from logic or reason. The implication is that campus leftists favor a set of principles that transcend ideology, for which the appropriate name is simply "social justice." Campus leftism is much more a matter of feeling than of thought and is based much more on passion or outrage than on reasoning. Thus rational counterarguments are often shouted down on the ground that they offend or discriminate against favored members of the campus community, while disfavored members of the community are allowed no sympathy if they claim to be offended or discriminated against.

Although it may seem pointless to look for intellectual content in campus leftism, it really is an ideology, and it has intellectual roots, no matter how shallow or seldom recognized they may be. Its guiding principle is the Marxist concept that people are divided into classes of oppressors and oppressed, each of which includes supporters of the oppressors or the oppressed. According to classical Marxism, the oppressors are the exploiting capitalist or landowning classes, who represent the "class enemy"; their victims are the working classes, otherwise known as "the people," with the implication that their class enemies are less than human. The oppressors must be resisted—and the oppressed defended—by any means necessary. While Stalin, Mao, and Pol Pot simply murdered large numbers of supposed oppressors, more moderate Marxists believed the job could be done by limiting the oppressors' legal rights, including their right to free speech. In the case of universities, in most Communist countries people from the wrong class background were either denied admission to higher education or allowed only restricted access to it, while those from the correct class backgrounds received preferential treatment in admissions and hiring.

As it happened, the American student radicals of the late sixties, who began the movement that evolved into today's campus leftism, found that most American factory workers and farmers were not the sort of oppressed class that classical Marxism had in mind. In the sixties the American working class was anti-Communist, socially conservative, mostly religious, not very dissatisfied, and not at all interested in political or social revolution. When the working class was added to the professional classes, the overwhelming majority of people in America turned out to be strongly opposed to Marxism, which professed to be supporting "the people." Blacks could be more plausibly identified as an oppressed class because most of them were poorer and had been subjected to various kinds of legal and social discrimination; but they seemed to have received legal equality under the Civil Rights Act of 1964, which also seemed to have granted legal equality to women. While most college students were so obviously privileged as to be hard to depict as economically oppressed, they were affected by the Vietnam War and the sexual revolution in ways that let them claim to be socially oppressed.

Because I was in college in the late sixties, I can attest that most college men at the time were afraid of being drafted, sent to Vietnam, and killed. Even if they had an exaggerated idea of their actual danger, their educational draft deferments were after all only deferments, and some of them really were drafted, sent to Vietnam, and killed.[3] Before the voting age was lowered from twenty-one to eighteen in 1971, most undergraduate students were ineligible to vote and could therefore claim that they had no say in the process that pursued the Vietnam War and administered the military draft. Many of them also decided that the war was unjust, because it pitted American oppressors and their Vietnamese collaborators against oppressed Vietnamese patriots. In a wider sense, the Vietnam War was part of a general conflict between Communism, which defended the rights of oppressed people everywhere, and America, which sided with the oppressors of the people. Consequently, student protests against the war were not merely self-serving but a struggle for social justice. The protesters insisted that the universities support their protests by banning ROTC programs and military research from campuses and by sponsoring antiwar speakers and "teach-ins."

For most students in the late sixties, going to college also meant experiencing the sexual revolution in full force. Though parental disapproval had often kept them from having sex in high school, college students who lived away from home were free from parental supervision. The parietal rules set by their colleges to discourage them from having sex were still resented but more or less ineffective. Reliable contraceptives were readily available. Most students soon decided that sex before marriage was entirely moral—at least under certain conditions, which they were sure that they satisfied. Whenever their sexual relationships went badly, as sexual relationships often do, the students usually blamed their parents and religions for making them feel guilty about what they assumed would otherwise have been wholly satisfactory experiences. The students also demanded that their colleges drop the rules designed to discourage sex among students and were soon demanding "coeducational" dormitories and bathrooms.

At the same time, largely through affirmative action programs, majority-white universities were admitting significant numbers of blacks for the first time. Quite a few of these black students were unhappy. They kept to themselves as much as possible and had trouble with their grades. Many of them insisted the problem was that universities were teaching a "white" or "Eurocentric" culture that was alien to blacks, and they demanded that the universities introduce "Afro-American" or "Afrocentric" programs that would represent black culture. Sometimes under the threat of violence, most colleges adopted such courses and majors, with overwhelmingly black enrollments and a large preponderance of excellent grades. White student radicals agreed that the existing "Eurocentric" college curriculum oppressed not only American blacks but all supposed victims of "imperialism," like Africans, Latin Americans, and Vietnamese. By extension, the curriculum oppressed all students, since they had either to learn it or to be punished by receiving bad grades. Student radicals also objected that what the curriculum taught was "irrelevant" to their concerns with war, race, and sex, accordingly demanding changes to make the "Eurocentric" and "elitist" curriculum "relevant" and "multicultural." Courses in "Western civilization" or "Western culture" were particular targets.

With help from a few Marxist professors and students, such ideas gradually coalesced into a radical movement that identified the oppressors and the oppressed in new ways. College students—though then mostly white, male, and from affluent families—were supposedly oppressed by being refused the vote, sent off to Vietnam to be killed, denied a fulfilling sex life, and indoctrinated in a culture that was the instrument of their oppression. Exactly who the oppressors were was somewhat less clear. Plainly the class enemies were older than the students and included most of their parents. While some students adopted the slogan, "Never trust anyone over thirty," this attacked a group that included some sympathetic professors and that some students dimly realized would in a few years include themselves. The oppressors definitely included the "military-industrial complex" (in the incautious words of President Eisenhower), which dominated America and had started the Vietnam War for obscure but surely nefarious reasons. The oppressors also included organized religion, which supported elite culture and tried to make the oppressed feel guilty about their sexual behavior. Yet the student radicalism of the sixties was a genuine mass movement, which no one precisely led. Despite some Marxists' efforts, few students took much interest in factory workers or the Soviet Union, though many professed to like Communist China, Cuba, and North Vietnam.

Most university administrators and professors, even if sometimes alarmed by student seizures of buildings and student strikes, felt at least partly sympathetic to student radicalism. They had already become disillusioned with the Vietnam War, which was going badly, and they had never liked policing sexual activity in university dormitories. Seeing what they taught attacked for its alleged lack of "relevance" was harder for them to accept, but most of them assumed that the students' demands could be accommodated by hiring a few new professors to teach a few new courses in a few new majors. Only a small minority of professors and administrators believed that student radicals should be firmly opposed. After all, most faculty and administrators thought that the young were the future, the future would be leftist and probably Marxist, there was indeed something seriously wrong with America (as the Vietnam War showed), and keeping up with the latest intellectual fashions was important.

Leftism and Postmodernism

The latest intellectual fashion was postmodernism (also known as poststructuralism), which questioned the existence of any objective truth.

But by no means did postmodernism imply that anyone's opinion was as good as anyone else's. Instead of facts, postmodernists spoke of "narratives" and "discourse," which were imposed by means of power, whether just or unjust. Oppressors tried to impose their own unjust narratives and discourse to serve their own evil interests, but the oppressed and their defenders could combat it with their own narratives and discourse, which since they were just could not be refuted by appeals to logical arguments or facts. In theory postmodernism could be applied to almost any topic, from climate change to ancient Greece, as long as someone could identify the classes of oppressors and oppressed and could either make analogies with present oppression or trace present injustices to past injustices. The oppressed were defined by the categories of race, class, and gender, and the forms of their oppression were defined as racism, imperialism, Eurocentrism, and patriarchy. While some postmodernists were not really radicals and some radicals were not really postmodernists, the two groups had much in common and were often allied.

What was theoretically interesting to followers of this developing ideology was the race, class, or gender group, not the individual. Groups were to be identified as oppressed or oppressive, and individuals were oppressed or oppressors when they were members or supporters of oppressed or oppressive groups. Even rich and educated blacks and women were still oppressed, because they suffered from racism and sexism in society, especially when they were unaware of it; even poor and uneducated whites and men were still classed as oppressors, because they failed to understand their own racism and sexism, especially if they thought they were not racist or sexist at all. The only way to escape the status of oppressor was to champion the rights of the oppressed even more passionately than the oppressed did themselves, and to identify new oppressed classes and ever more subtle forms of oppression. The original oppressed groups were college students and blacks, but women, Hispanics, and members of non-Western cultures were soon added. Homosexuals, transsexuals, the disabled, animals, and others were added somewhat later, stigmatizing their corresponding oppressors as "heteronormativists," "binarists," "ableists," and "speciesists," respectively.

Meanwhile, the expansion of the American academic job market that had begun with the GI Bill ended around 1970 when college enrollments stopped growing as the last baby boomers were admitted. Universities now needed to hire few if any more faculty after years of hiring many young professors who would remain employed for decades; the only professors who were retiring were the few who had been hired in the thirties, when enrollments had been far smaller and money to hire professors had been short. The drastic fall in available jobs coincided with the beginning of affirmative action in academic hiring. Because most professors agreed that universities should be opened to blacks, women, and new ideas, most of the few available positions went either to black or female applicants, or, especially since there were so few blacks with degrees to hire, to postmodernists and radicals. New positions that could not be justified by growing enrollments could be justified by a need to hire more blacks and women, or to teach ethnic or postmodern courses. Hiring committees overwhelmed by too many applications could avoid examining most of the applicants' credentials simply by identifying and hiring blacks, women, or postmodernists. Similar hiring practices continue today. They have resulted in steadily more left-wing faculties and—since most administrators are just professors uninterested in teaching and research—more left-wing administrations.

The paradigm of oppressors and oppressed spread through almost every field in the humanities and to some fields in the sciences. The oppressors were identified as Europeans and white Americans, capitalists, "elitists," men, and heterosexuals. Postmodernism meant that all contrary facts could be dismissed as attempts to enforce oppression. The works of Homer, the Greek dramatists, and Shakespeare were considered "elitist" literature, even though their original audiences came from every level of society and were largely illiterate. The quality of literature or art was considered uninteresting unless it illustrated oppression or resistance to oppression. Aristotle was said to have stolen his philosophy from the Library of Alexandria that had supposedly been founded by black Africans, even though the library had been founded by white Greeks after Aristotle's death.[4] Other creations of leftist scholarship included the elements of "multiculturalism" already mentioned, such as a feminist Africa, a pacifist Islam, and an evil United States and Western Europe. Research that failed to fit the paradigm was dismissed as outdated and irrelevant. At a lecture I once attended about Bermuda, a questioner criticized the lecturer for ignoring its colonists' oppression of native

Bermudans and remained indignant even after hearing that Bermuda was uninhabited before the colonists came.

Campus leftism became much less concerned with helping the supposedly oppressed than with demonizing the supposed oppressors. The allegedly oppressed who failed to recognize their oppression, like women who wanted to assume traditional roles as wives and mothers, were lectured on their need for "raised consciousness." Radical white professors sometimes needed to teach minority students to recognize seemingly inoffensive remarks and actions as "microaggressions" to be resented. Yet anyone with a real concern for the interests of women and minorities should realize that telling them to be outraged even by a Halloween costume or the name of a football team will discourage them from trying to help themselves and encourage them to antagonize people who would otherwise be sympathetic to them. Anyone with a real concern for blacks should want police protection for the many blacks in danger of being terrorized and murdered by black criminals. Anyone with a real concern for people confused about their sexuality should be reluctant to encourage them to choose homosexuality or transsexuality, let alone to undergo drastic and largely irreversible surgery. Nonetheless, the question of whether leftist social engineering causes more misery than it relieves is irrelevant if the only permissible motive is to combat supposed oppressors and to defend the identities of the supposedly oppressed.

The paradigm of oppressors and oppressed explains some combinations of dogmas that can otherwise seem logically inconsistent. It seems bizarre to insist that sexual orientation cannot be chosen but gender can; but both positions serve to stigmatize as unjust and oppressive the conservative and religious views that homosexuality and transsexuality are unnatural. Animal rights are important if the animals are oppressed by traditionalists and capitalists; but a right to life for an unborn child can be ignored if oppressive religious traditionalists defend it. Because only women have abortions, women's equality requires a right to abortion for any purpose including mere convenience—except sex selection for boys, which even if women want it depends on male oppression. That American blacks are almost six times more likely to be imprisoned than whites is a scandal because blacks are oppressed and whites are oppressors; but that men are almost fourteen times more likely to be imprisoned than women is no problem, because men are oppressors and women are oppressed. That a white policeman in Ferguson, Missouri, killed a black thief who was trying to take his gun away (presumably to kill him) is an injustice, because whites are oppressors and blacks oppressed. The only acceptable remedies for global warming are those that penalize oppressors, especially capitalists, and certainly not nuclear power, which enriches capitalists, or climate engineering, which might not penalize them.

Campus ideology is, however, not very interested in defining exactly who belongs to the predetermined classes of oppressors and oppressed. Questioning someone's claim to be oppressed is condemned as "blaming the victim," while claiming not to be an oppressor is condemned as insensitivity to oppression. The status of oppressor or oppressed can be inherited, but only by groups as groups. Most white Americans have no slaveholding ancestors while most black Americans probably do, and many black Americans are richer than many white Americans; but all whites are still considered more privileged than all blacks. Homosexuality and transsexuality are supposed to be a source of pride, but heterosexuality is not, because homosexuals and transsexuals are oppressed and heterosexuals are oppressors. Even though campus leftism was originally not much interested in homosexuals and transsexuals, now everyone must approve of all homosexual or transsexual behavior, even if it would be considered cruel, reckless, offensive, or criminal if practiced by heterosexuals. For example, homosexual rape is a subject of little concern to campus leftists, and the reason is not that it seldom happens. A man who has hundreds of callous and casual liaisons with women can be denounced as a sexual predator; but if he has such liaisons with men, that is just his identity ("who I am").

While such beliefs have become increasingly influential off campus, on most campuses they have come to be not merely influential but incontestable, to the point where any questioning of them is taken as clear proof of racism, sexism, or homophobia. Subjects for courses or research unrelated to oppression are dismissed out of hand; the paradigm of oppressors and oppressed cannot be challenged, and even the paradigm's applicability to specific cases is dangerous to discuss. According to campus leftists, universities' only legitimate function is to teach and produce leftist propaganda and to prohibit criticizing it.

The idea of a kind of affirmative action to hire moderate or conservative professors is condemned for treating oppressors as if they were oppressed. Even if this sort of affirmative action did help a few moderate or conservative professors get jobs, it would still leave them with no useful role to play on campus, vilified by many of their colleagues and students and ignored by most of the rest. Similarly, the efforts of some foundations and other organizations to support moderate and conservative professors and students may help their morale a bit, but will do nothing to restore free speech on campus. If others have created their identities among the oppressed by demonizing you as an oppressor, nothing you can tell them will help. Speaking out will only keep you from being hired, given tenure, or promoted. It can also make your life on campus almost intolerable.

To be sure, in most universities the majority of professors and administrators are not dogmatic leftists and are to varying degrees distressed by the excesses of campus leftism. But very few of the more moderate professors and administrators will speak forthrightly against those excesses. There are several reasons for this. One reason is fear of retaliation, even if only in the form of a colleague's outburst over lunch at the faculty club. Another reason is an often justified feeling that speaking out will do no good and will probably make things worse. Still another reason is a feeling that campus leftism, though it may sometimes have gone too far, is "on the right side of history," defending people who really have been oppressed and attacking people who really have been insensitive toward the oppressed or have actively oppressed them, including some truly bigoted people. For such reasons the postmodernists and leftists were hired in the first place by professors and administrators who were much more moderate than the people they hired. Nonetheless, many of these relatively moderate professors and administrators have now come to realize that the universities have become hostile to academic freedom as they used to know it and to teaching many works and ideas that they value. They worry most of all when they see moderate colleagues (or themselves) being viciously accused of racism, sexism, or homophobia. Under certain circumstances they might say something. But probably not. Who wants to be on the wrong side of history?

Outside the universities the problem is still not as bad as it is within them, although many Democrats have obviously become worried about not showing quite enough vehemence in denouncing supposed oppressors. Even Sanders has sometimes failed to satisfy the demands of his student supporters. People in less monolithically leftist professions than college teaching, particularly politicians, usually try to be more careful about demonizing large groups of people, who after all are potential or actual voters, customers, coworkers, or friends. Part of the reason our national economic policies remain saner than our foreign or social policies is that economics departments are the main parts of our universities that still have some moderate and conservative professors. Yet many ideas that would have been considered absurd a short time ago have gone straight from the universities to become public policies enforced by the federal government and defended by most Democratic politicians. With the increasing polarization of American society, those on the left often find themselves pushed into positions that they would recently have considered too extreme. Such positions should be firmly combated, especially with a reasoned argument that demonizing men, whites, conservatives, and religious believers as oppressors is not social justice but bigotry. Unfortunately, the people who now dominate our universities have little interest in reasoned arguments.

Chapter 4

WHAT IS GOOD TEACHING?

Students Grading Professors

When I attended my sister's college graduation at Stanford in 1978, the ceremonies included an award for Professor of the Year. The winner, apparently chosen in a poll of all students, was an affable fellow who taught what was then Stanford's most popular course, on human sexuality. The student who introduced him implied that his course was highly entertaining and assured us that the professor taught his students not just about sex but about life. Bearded, balding, and a bit chubby, the professor had something of the guru about him, but with none of the pretentiousness or solemnity of most gurus. His amusing acceptance speech showed that he was very good at communicating with students, and though in it he said nothing much about his subject—he mostly told jokes—I was convinced that his course offered not just entertainment but useful information. Yet as I listened to him, I could hardly help wondering whether other Stanford professors, teaching courses on topics like calculus, philosophy of mind, or Chinese, were not showing greater skill than his in conveying material that their students found intrinsically less interesting or accessible than human sexuality. And if those professors were doing that, were they not better teachers than he was, and did they not deserve to be named Professor of the Year more than he did?

A few years ago, at Saint Louis University (SLU), I was invited to the ceremonial dinner at which undergraduate teaching awards were given because I was one of the professors who had been nominated for a teaching award, though I fell short actually of winning one. Being nominated turned out not to be much of an honor, since around a hundred professors were present and about twenty awards were given. After dinner each award was presented by the students, who read a selection of the student comments that had led to the professor's being chosen; the professor then accepted the award with a few words of thanks. To the best of my recollection, during the whole evening just one of the student comments referred to the academic content of the professor's teaching. (That comment was about one of my colleagues in the history department.) The others emphasized how much fun the classes were, how nice the professors were, how the professors told entertaining stories and good jokes, and how they drank beer and talked sports with their students outside class. The professor who won the award for the *very* best teacher, a warm and fuzzy character not unlike the winner at Stanford, was praised above all because toward the end of each semester he invited all his students to his house and cooked them a delicious dinner. Someone must have mentioned what subject he taught, but no one seemed interested in it and it escapes me now. (Psychology, perhaps? Anyway, not cooking.) I found the occasion profoundly discouraging, and when I was invited the next year I sent my regrets.

More recently a dean emailed me that I had been nominated for a graduate advising award. I was flattered until I discovered that in order to be considered I would need to solicit testimonials from all my graduate advisees. I immediately took myself out of contention. I explained that my advisees were dependent on me not only for advice but for grades and letters of recommendation for jobs and fellowships, and I considered it unethical to ask them to recommend me when they could reasonably fear that I would be less enthusiastic about them if they were not enthusiastic about me. I suggested that in the future the dean should ask graduate students for confidential evaluations of their advisers, whether positive, negative, or mixed, and give advising awards on the basis of those comments. The dean and my departmental chairman seemed astonished. Some money went with the award—I never learned how much—and here I was refusing even to be considered, on grounds that they had never thought of or heard of from anyone else.[1] Before this I had assumed that the undergraduate teaching awards had been given on the basis of students' usual teaching evaluations, but now I was less sure, especially because the evaluation forms never ask about such things as whether the professor invited you to dinner. Possibly those finalists had been required to solicit testimonials as well. I decided not to ask; I had already made enough trouble.

At the great majority of American universities today, teaching, both undergraduate and graduate, is judged primarily or exclusively on the basis of student teaching evaluations. This system invites corruption and results in it. Student evaluations admittedly have their uses. I read my students' evaluations with interest, and not only because they affect my salary. I am gratified by the favorable ones, which are most of them. I never take too seriously the occasional complaints about the heaviness of the workload and the difficulty of the grading, though I would begin to worry if I received such complaints from most students in a good class, because to make demands too far above prevailing standards seems unfair. I have also received several suggestions for improvements that I adopted over the years. For example, I got so many complaints after assigning Machiavelli's *History of Florence* at Hillsdale and Tacitus's *Annals* at FIU (in both cases the students were disoriented by the authors' irony) that I replaced them on my reading lists with Guicciardini's *History of Italy* and Suetonius's *Twelve Caesars* (though I kept Tacitus for graduate students, who were able to handle him). As a rule, a professor who receives many unfavorable student evaluations is probably doing something wrong; but a professor who receives many favorable evaluations may just be an easy grader or an accomplished raconteur and not a good teacher at all.

You can see a good sampling of candid student evaluations on the website Ratemyprofessors.com, which only includes ratings from students who access it. Notice how many highly rated professors score high on "easiness," which is always assumed to be a virtue. Note also that the chili pepper symbol for "hotness" just means that the professor is physically attractive.[2] The disillusioned former Harvard dean Harry Lewis makes a refreshing comment about student evaluations:

> Two Harvard psychologists showed that the numbers students assign lecturers after watching only thirty seconds of video with no sound correlate very highly with student evaluations of the entire course at

the end of the term. Students watching the brief videos had no information about what the instructors were saying and ranked instructors
on personality traits such as optimism and confidence, not on teaching
quality. This experiment conclusively establishes that student course
evaluations are simply consumer preference metrics of the shallowest
sort.[3]

That conclusion may be a little too definite—a few students do make
thoughtful comments—but only a little.

I have never tried assigning little or no work and giving all my
students As, but three times my course ratings were considerably lower
than usual. I usually handed out the evaluation forms in the next-to-last
class, but once at SLU the forms were not ready until the last day, when
three students who usually skipped class came to pick up their graded
term papers. They seem not to have liked their low grades and made
unfavorable comments on the course, which otherwise they had hardly
ever attended. Another time an administrative error allowed a student to
fill out an evaluation form after he had already received his final grade,
an F. He had missed almost every class but submitted apparently valid
medical excuses; I told him I never counted off for missed classes but
advised him to drop the course because he had missed too much of it.
Later he sent me a long email complaining about his F, which had prevented him from graduating on time, and declaring that he had learned
nothing from my class (which his final exam showed to be approximately
correct). His comment on the evaluation form was easily identifiable: in
it he complained about his F, and he was the only student who failed. In
a class of ten, a single zero (on a scale of five points) has a major effect
on the average course rating. If you think my student had a right to his
opinion, you should perhaps consider that he had attended scarcely any
of the course he was judging.

A third time when my ratings were lower than usual was a class
in Greek history at FIU. In a discussion of Thucydides's *History of the
Peloponnesian War*, I asked the class whether the Spartans were right
that the Athenian empire, originally a confederacy of cities for mutual
defense, had become a "tyranny" by the time of the Peloponnesian War.
There were about twenty in the class, of whom about six dominated the
discussion. All of them agreed that the Athenian empire was indeed a

tyranny, because when the city of Mytilene tried to secede, the Athenians besieged and conquered it. This is a perfectly defensible opinion, but I wanted to show that another opinion was also possible. I pointed out that most Athenian cities never tried to secede and that Mytilene, unlike most member cities, was an aristocracy, which surrendered only after its common people refused to fight the Athenians. The students insisted that this was irrelevant: How could the cities possibly be free if they were unable to leave the empire freely? I pointed out that in 1861 our own state of Florida had seceded from the United States, which attacked it and forced it back into the Union. Did this mean that *we* were not free? The class fell silent. My remark, which had been meant to keep the discussion going, killed it completely. My evaluations for that course included several criticisms of my lack of respect for student opinions. Ever since, I have tried not to make similarly devastating arguments in class discussions.

This incident raises a subtler question about student evaluations than whether they can be bought by easy assignments and easy grading. Evaluations conducted by colleges and universities create an atmosphere in which students' opinions are given more respect than is always good for their education. In high school, college, and graduate school, my own best teachers repeatedly challenged my opinions and sometimes ridiculed them, not necessarily to make me abandon them but to make me defend them more methodically and to revise them if they were inadequately thought out. If a few of my teachers sometimes carried this practice too far and were needlessly harsh, they did me no real harm and probably did me some good. If now I deliberately avoid challenging my students' opinions as much as my best teachers did—and I regret to say that I do—the reason is that I need to teach my students as they are, and my ability to teach them is reduced if they are alienated, as my students in that class at FIU were. This is a general problem, aggravated by official student evaluations but chiefly caused by the widespread attitude that students are "consumers" who need to be kept happy with the "product" they are buying from their professors—which is an enjoyable experience taking the course, not a rigorous education. Yet students should realize that the best professors are not always the nicest ones.

Unofficial student evaluations, like those on Ratemyprofessors.com, do no such damage. There students feel free to say, as some do, "Sign up for this prof! I never went to class or cracked a book all semester, and got an A!" Students who write or read such an "evaluation" have no illusions that it really evaluates the course or the professor. They know that the course and the professor taught nothing to students who never went to class or did any of the reading. Students never write such things on official evaluations, because they know that they could harm the professor's reputation and jeopardize future easy As for themselves and others. Why deans and departmental chairmen who are supposed to evaluate teaching seldom look for comments like this on Ratemyprofessors.com, or at least seem never to hold such comments against professors, is an interesting question. One might also ask why administrators almost never compute the average grades that professors give to see whether they nearly always give As and never give Fs. Another relevant question is why administrators who are supposed to evaluate teaching scarcely ever visit classrooms to watch the teaching being done. Instead, student teaching evaluations are used as almost the sole criterion for judging teaching, and no one bothers to ask what they mean.

Some defenders of student evaluations insist that "there is *no* consistent correlation between the grades a faculty member gives and the ratings he or she receives from a well-designed student rating form" (emphasis in original). Yet the same defender of student course evaluations acknowledges the clear evidence that lower-level courses receive lower ratings than upper-level ones, required courses receive lower ratings than electives, and courses in the natural sciences and mathematics receive lower ratings than courses in the humanities and social sciences.[4] This difference is unlikely to reflect worse teaching, since most professors teach both lower-level and upper-level courses and both required and elective courses. Scores on Graduate Record Examinations (GREs), which are taken by college seniors who plan to apply to graduate school, indicate that colleges are actually doing a better job of teaching students in the natural sciences and mathematics than in the social sciences and humanities.[5] The reason for the difference in ratings is much more likely to be that, regardless of the quality of teaching, most students are more interested in their upper-level and elective courses than in their lower-level and required courses, and they find courses in the humanities and social sciences easier than those in the natural sciences and mathematics.

The alleged absence of correlation between grades and ratings need not mean that professors cannot buy better student ratings with easy grading, but only that average student evaluations, most of which are favorable anyway, combine ratings given for different reasons. A course may have favorable ratings because it really is good or because it is easy (or possibly both); a course may have unfavorable ratings because it really is bad or because it is hard (or possibly both). I suspect, however, that very few courses get unfavorable ratings because they are too easy. Ratings given by students who never attend class and never do the assigned work are obviously worthless, whether favorable or unfavorable. Other factors, such as the likability of the professor and the intrinsic interest of the subject, also figure into the ratings. But students cannot learn anything from a course if they never attend it and never do the reading for it, and they cannot learn much from a course if they seldom attend it and do little of the reading for it. They also learn little or nothing from submitting a bad or plagiarized term paper, as most of the worst students do. The answer to people who say a course can be both good and easy is that, for most students, a really easy course is one in which they do almost no work and learn almost nothing. Professors who get favorable ratings from students whom they give As for no attendance and no work are guilty of bribery and should be dismissed, not rewarded, as they now nearly always are.

The Elusive Criteria

My experience as an undergraduate at Harvard contradicted several of the clichés that are commonly repeated about teaching. Having graduate students teach undergraduates is often considered an abuse, but two of the three best courses I took as an undergraduate were taught by advanced graduate students, who were brilliant and enthusiastic. The third was taught by a brilliant and enthusiastic senior professor, the classicist John Finley, but two of the three worst courses I took were taught by senior professors (and the third by a bored graduate student). One senior professor, the biologist James D. Watson, may well have deserved his Nobel Prize in Medicine (I certainly cannot judge) and wrote a good textbook that was used in the class he gave; but he was a disorganized and almost incomprehensible lecturer who was wasted teaching an undergraduate course for non-scientists. The other senior professor, Robert Lee Wolff, taught Byzantine history from ancient notes he had largely cribbed almost verbatim from published sources; he never published a book on Byzantium and was clearly less interested in it than in the modern Balkans and Victorian novels (on which he did publish books). One might think that a good professor is one who persuades students to go into his field; but I became a Byzantine historian in spite of Wolff's course. I also know students who have been inspired to go into a field by a charismatic professor who "made the subject come alive," only to discover later that they had no real interest in or talent for it. In such cases, the professors did their students no favor.

Like most professors and administrators, I have little direct evidence for how my colleagues teach. But much of the evidence I do have is disturbing. Many professors resist the idea of letting colleagues or administrators attend their classes and refuse permission to have their classes tape-recorded or filmed by students. To judge from the complaints I receive from my students who never go to class and never learn the material but expect not just passing grades but good ones, many professors give good grades for little or no work. Many of my students also express surprise that I never give multiple-choice or true-false tests or that I "line-edit" their papers, correcting spelling, grammar, infelicities of expression, and minor factual errors. Evidently many professors do give multiple-choice tests and neither correct papers nor in some cases even comment on them. My students are sometimes embarrassingly laudatory in their evaluations of what I think should be normal good teaching. I notice on Ratemyprofessors.com that a number of top-rated professors show cartoons in class and assign comic books and video games. I am also troubled by what I find written on blackboards, whiteboards, or sheets for overhead projectors from classes held before mine: simplistic outlines full of generalities on subjects like the effects of racism or the causes of American imperialism, often containing misspellings, blatant bias, and factual errors. This sort of evidence, though not necessarily this sort of teaching, has become less common with the increasing use of PowerPoint.

I first learned about PowerPoint from a lecture promoting it at FIU. I still regret not having told the lecturer during the discussion afterward that it was one of the worst lectures I had ever heard, full of irrelevant images and conveying no coherent information. While PowerPoint is clearly needed for some subjects (with the demise of slide projectors, my wife uses it for all her art history lectures), I have never used it, having learned long ago that when I showed slides many students stopped listening to what I said and paid attention only to the pictures. A recent and perceptive book on the problems of higher education includes three suggestions for improving teaching, including "Stop Powerpointing," because "files of slides etch the day's outline in stone; new ideas can't be added, as they can on a chalkboard." Another suggestion, "Preventing Plagiarism," is obvious but sound and not hard to implement. After SLU dropped its subscription to the effective plagiarism detector Turnitin because it cost money and students complained about it, I returned to my old practice of requiring submission of a rough draft of each paper (which I look at without grading it) before the final draft. The third suggestion is "Monitor Laptops," because "in almost all the classes we attended, at least half the screens displayed games of solitaire, reruns of sporting events, messages to friends."[6] This problem is real, but I remain reluctant to adopt the suggested solution because a professor who walks around the classroom monitoring laptops cannot concentrate on teaching, and laptops are convenient for taking notes and letting students introduce new facts into discussions. After all, though students might mistakenly think that they learn something from a superficial PowerPoint presentation, they know that they learn nothing from playing solitaire. If they never learn the material, I can find out on the examinations and give them low grades.

The real reason that grade inflation is a serious problem, and that those who consider it unimportant are wrong, is that grading is almost the only way to make sure that students do the assigned work and learn something.[7] The majority of students will do the least work for which they think they can get an acceptable grade. If a superficial knowledge of the material, or no knowledge at all, will get them the grade they want, that is all they will bother to acquire. (Graduate student grades are somewhat different, because graduate students need their professors' recommendations more than grades, and they must worry that if they do poor work those recommendations might lack the customary enthusiasm.) Even some quite responsible students with busy schedules and other, more difficult classes will spend little time on a class if they know they are assured of a good grade in it. Only a small minority of students will do all the assigned work just because they are interested in it, especially because many courses include reading, problem sets, or laboratory assignments that are important for understanding the subject but not very interesting in themselves.

The idea that a good professor can make any material seem interesting is almost as silly as the idea that a good professor can make calculus seem as interesting as human sexuality. In a lecture one can make a subject sound more interesting than it really is by misrepresenting it, but misrepresenting anything is bad teaching. The truth is that some subjects are inherently less interesting than others for just about everyone. Samuel Johnson wrote of Milton's *Paradise Lost* (which he admired), "None ever wished it longer than it is." The same is true of the conjugations of Greek verbs, the declensions of Latin nouns, and a great deal of other academic material, especially in mathematics and the natural sciences. Though I am presumably much more interested in English, Greek, and Latin literature than the average college student is, I remain grateful that I read *Paradise Lost* and learned Greek and Latin grammar in classes, because I doubt I would have had the perseverance to do any of those things properly on my own. (Perhaps I should also have taken a course that required me to read Joyce's *Ulysses*, which I never have had the patience to read on my own. Of course, not everything hard to do is worth doing.) Most students, if they know the alternative is a poor grade on their transcript, will do the assigned work, and in the process may well discover why the work is important and find it rewarding. Just lowering the grade for each missed class is pointless, because many students will show up and play solitaire, text, or daydream. The only effective enforcement is to read papers and examinations carefully, giving the good ones high grades and the poor ones low grades.

Thus grade inflation is bad for several serious reasons. It discourages learning; it allows professors to bribe students to give them better evaluations than they would otherwise receive; it unfairly penalizes the students of professors whose grades are less inflated; and it encourages students to choose classes not for their educational value but for their easy grading. The consensus among professors and administrators is that grade inflation is not good but that nothing much can or should be done about it.[8] After all, students might be getting better, teaching might be getting better, we want students to concentrate on learning rather than grades, and we want to encourage struggling students by giving them good grades even when they learn little or nothing. (Notice that this last argument, which is probably the most prevalent but seldom voiced explicitly, is inconsistent with the other three arguments.) Besides, professors must be free to grade as they wish. Moreover, the best minds in American higher education have been unable to arrive at any practical way to halt grade inflation. Lewis, the former Harvard dean, asserts, "The most effective way to combat rising grades would be to initiate serious conversations, at the departmental level, about what constitutes A, B, and C work—'therapy,' as a colleague called it, rather than regulation."[9] Whenever an academic administrator talks about "initiating serious conversations" or "therapy," you can be fairly sure nothing effective will be done.

The best minds in higher education should think harder about grade inflation. Since almost all grades are now entered online, it should be easy to compile a cumulative average of each professor's grades. With a little more calculation, each grade in a professor's class could be compared to the cumulative grade point averages of the students in that class. If, for example, a professor gives grades that average 4.25 (A−) to a class of students with overall grade point averages of 3.25 (B−), we can be pretty sure that the professor is an unusually easy grader. If administrators want to reduce grade inflation, they can first send every professor the number (positive or negative) showing the difference between the average grades he has given his undergraduates in the past and the same undergraduates' grade point averages. The administration can then announce that next year, after the first tenth of a point that a professor's grades exceed his students' grade point averages, for each additional tenth of a point the professor's annual raise will be reduced by 10 percent. Though such numbers may seem arbitrary, they are far more objective than student evaluation scores. Something like this procedure would exert strong pressure on grade inflation. This would in turn make grades more reliable, improve students' education, and reduce a source of corruption that benefits lazy professors and lazy students at the expense of conscientious professors and conscientious students. Yet I doubt that anything of the sort will be widely adopted; such corruption is too deeply ingrained in today's colleges and universities.

Many people think that online education ("distance learning") has the potential to revolutionize higher education, allowing students to take courses from the best professors in the world at scarcely any cost. These predictions seem to me to overestimate students' self-discipline. In theory, a lecture that you can watch whenever you like, as often as you like, is splendid. Likewise, in theory you could turn students loose in a good library and let them read there for four years and emerge with an excellent education. In practice, most students who attend universities today, like almost all of us, tend to postpone things they can do anytime, especially things they are not eager to do anyway. They also tend to listen more carefully to a professor who is actually present and looking at them, even in a large classroom, than to images and voices from a screen. Today not listening carefully to an online lecture means texting, talking, playing video games, and doing many other things that make paying adequate attention impossible. Taking careful notes, which is usually a crucial part of paying full attention to a lecture, seems hardly worth doing when you can listen to the lecture again anytime. Discussions, again, are much more involving and helpful in a small group in person than online.[10] Consequently, many students never even finish courses that they take online, and if they say they have finished, any rigorous test will show that most of them have learned less than they would from a regular course. The temptation to give extremely easy tests to such students, or to allow them to cheat on the tests in the absence of adequate proctoring, is correspondingly great.

No doubt various methods can be used to mitigate these disadvantages of online courses. For example, students can be allowed to listen to a lecture only when it is actually being delivered by the professor; but then many expensively equipped studios are needed to allow many professors to lecture at the same time, and the students lose any advantages of being able to hear lectures over again. Besides, students may well ask why they should listen to their own professor lecture when a better lecture by a more famous professor is available online on the same subject. Similarly, technology can allow the professor to see the students' faces in many small windows on a computer screen, but any professor who tries to pay attention to all the windows is going to be constantly distracted from teaching. Combining screens can make it possible for the professor and students to hold discussion sessions; but the discussions will be awkward and cumbersome, and most of the students will have trouble paying attention to them. Attentive professors may be able to see enough of their students to make it hard for them to cheat on examinations, but what about crib sheets positioned above the computer screen or a friend supplying information from behind the screen? Examinations can be proctored in a classroom by graduate students, but then why not have the graduate students teach the whole course in the classroom? This sort of online course is likely to use very expensive technology to deliver an inferior education—except possibly when it replaces a giant lecture course in a huge auditorium, where the professor and students hardly interact anyway.

A new study by the Brookings Institution has compared over 750 online and in-person courses in some 168,000 sections taken by over 230,000 students at for-profit DeVry University. These online and in-person courses were "identical in most ways," with the same syllabuses, textbooks, assignments, quizzes, examinations, and grading norms, and often the same professors. Yet the online students received grades that were on average 0.44 points lower than the in-person students, for an average of a C rather than a B−; the grades of the bottom 10 percent of students averaged 0.8 points lower. Moreover, the online students who took courses in the same subject the next term received grades that were 0.42 points lower than those of the in-person students, and the students who took a course online were 9 percent more likely to drop out of the university.[11] These are terrible results for courses that in all probability are of poor quality anyway, since DeVry University has a bad reputation and has been plagued by lawsuits for deceptive advertising.[12] Because of such results, online education has failed to take the academic world by storm so far, and will probably fail to dominate it in the future, except perhaps as a low-quality substitute for low-quality courses.[13]

Certainly an online course from which students learn nothing can be cheaper than a regular course from which students learn nothing, but for students to learn nothing from taking no course at all is still cheaper, and equally valuable. The interest in online education in universities today is in part a sign of indifference to whether students learn anything or not. Another factor is probably that online education has the enthusiastic support of the computer scientists who design online courses in computer science. Those professors are teaching material that is uniquely suited to computers, are often obsessively interested in their material, and are sometimes asocial people who prefer to study without human contact. Online courses may actually be an effective way of teaching computer science to enthusiastic computer scientists and computer science students, though not necessarily to the rest of us, who often need our questions about computers to be answered by human beings in person. In any case, the methods of online computer science courses are much less suitable for other fields that are less easily reduced to indisputable facts and for less obsessive students who need frequent guidance from their professors. Like many ways of saving money in academics, online courses sacrifice quality at a time when the average quality of courses is already low.

Elements of Good Teaching

What, then, is the best way to improve college teaching? Some people, especially professors of education, think that much more attention should be paid to training graduate students to teach, thus supplying them with skills that will supposedly make them better teachers throughout their careers as professors (if they should be lucky enough to have such careers). The same attitude leads professors of education to think that what high school teachers need most is training in teaching, not training in the subjects they will teach, with the result that many high school teachers use the latest methods to teach their subjects poorly. Most graduate students receive some training in teaching now, usually from working as teaching assistants with senior professors and often from formal teaching colloquia. A little such training is unlikely to do them much harm, unless it convinces them to rely heavily on PowerPoint and simplistic outlines. A few basic skills are equally applicable to teaching almost all subjects and can be taught, more or less: speak clearly and audibly, prepare your classes carefully, organize your material coherently without oversimplifying, avoid overestimating or underestimating your students' knowledge or abilities, and tell relevant jokes when possible. Beyond such basics, however, being an effective teacher of science, mathematics, languages, history, philosophy, or literature requires very different skills.

The best basic training for teaching any subject is taking good undergraduate and graduate courses in it, then emulating what you found to work best in those courses and avoiding what you found to work badly. The best advanced training in teaching is to teach your own courses conscientiously and to refine your knowledge of what works by trial and error. Teaching evaluations can be of some use for this purpose, though those on Ratemyprofessors.com are likely to be more useful than those on official university evaluation forms, because only the former will show when some of the requirements are too easy. A certain degree of empathy is also helpful in teaching, but it cannot really be taught to people who lack it. Still, any but the borderline autistic should be able to master the social skills needed to be effective teachers if they try. They can however avoid trying if they rely on easy grading, which will give them acceptable evaluations without effective teaching, just as it gives their students acceptable grades without effective learning. (A satisfactory knowledge of English is also essential but is sometimes not possessed by graduate students from foreign countries, who should not be allowed to teach until they have demonstrated such knowledge to their supervisors.)

Although good teaching skills are useful for effective teaching, they are also quite compatible with ineffective or bad teaching. This may seem paradoxical to those whose ideas of good teaching go back to primary or secondary school or to introductory survey courses in college. Teaching skills may well be the decisive factor in determining whether you are an effective teacher of elementary subjects like reading or beginning algebra. There is little dispute about what makes up a basic knowledge of reading or algebra, or that these are things all students need to learn. Drawing up standardized tests for such subjects is a relatively straightforward task, and most people are unimpressed by the excuses made by teachers whose students do badly on such tests after taking their courses and getting good grades. Most (though not all) of the teachers of these subjects know enough to teach beginning students how to read or how to do algebra. If these teachers fail, they are probably failing as teachers— for example, by not preparing their classes carefully, or by overestimating or underestimating their students' abilities. Yet the large number of college students who cheerfully learn next to nothing mostly take courses from professors who speak clearly and audibly, organize their material coherently, and practice other basic teaching skills. If professors neglect such things, they usually get complaints on their teaching evaluations. Yet they can do all these things, receive laudatory teaching evaluations, and still teach their students nothing of value.

To begin with, brilliantly taught courses can be worthless. In a celebrated experiment done in 1972, an actor "who looked distinguished and sounded authoritative" was hired to impersonate the fictitious "Dr. Myron L. Fox, an authority on the application of mathematics to human behavior," and to deliver a lecture on "Mathematical Game Theory as Applied to Physician Education" before three different audiences of psychiatrists, psychologists, social workers, teachers, and administrators. The lecturer was told to make his lecture and his answers to questions a farrago of "double talk, neologisms, non sequiturs and contradictory statements...interspersed with parenthetical humor and meaningless references to unrelated topics." On a questionnaire given to the fifty-five members of all three audiences, favorable responses heavily outnumbered negative responses, except that a significant minority thought "Dr. Fox" tended to dwell on "the obvious" (though most of what he said was actually nonsense) and just one respondent claimed to have read his publications (which did not exist). "Dr. Fox" was praised for his interest in his subject, the examples he used to clarify his material, his well-organized presentation, and being stimulating and interesting.[14] If these were the responses of people who had professional expertise to help them evaluate a lecture that was carefully designed to be meaningless, how reliable are undergraduate teaching evaluations? For that matter, how valuable for determining whether job candidates are good teachers—let alone good scholars—are lectures given during on-campus interviews to professors who are not specialists in the candidate's subject?

These questions are particularly pertinent when the teacher is a postmodernist, Marxist, feminist, or partisan of some other ideology to whom theory or ideology (or fashionability) is more important than accuracy and who may even deny that facts can exist independently of interpretation. The danger of bias is a real one, and may well be worse if the teacher's ideology is not overt. Students are duly warned if the professor says, "As a Marxist, I endorse this interpretation, but non-Marxists have different interpretations, which I consider mistaken for the following reasons." (I adopt a similar approach when I teach subjects on which I disagree with Marxists or postmodernists, describing their views and explaining why I disagree with them.) What happens more often is that a professor teaches the ideological interpretations he favors as if they were accepted by every current authority on the subject, which in some fields in the humanities and social sciences can be very nearly true. Perhaps worse yet is the fact that most ideologues frame the subjects of their courses in an ideological way. No doubt the history and literature of sexuality, workers, women, and racial minorities—and race, class, and gender in general—are legitimate subjects for courses. But in many American university departments such subjects are crowding out everything else, not only in specialized courses but in the few general surveys that remain. Courses called World History or Introduction to English Literature can be almost entirely about race, class, and gender. Yet many students like such courses because they are often taught with enthusiasm and have clear demands. You can easily pick up the ideology and its related jargon, apply it to examinations and papers, and be rewarded with an A.

A related problem is that so many professors offer and require specialized courses rather than general surveys or introductions to the subject. Since most professors have written a highly specialized dissertation and continue to do similarly specialized research throughout their careers, few of them want to teach courses that give a comprehensive and balanced treatment of their entire field, which would include many aspects of it that they find unfamiliar or uninteresting. The easiest way to make sure that nobody needs to teach a course that he finds uninteresting and that everyone has enough students for the courses that do interest him is to require students to take not survey courses but a range of courses in the different professors' specialties. This is the "pork barrel principle" for distribution requirements identified long ago by the sociologists Christopher Jencks and David Riesman.[15] The practice is hard to stop, especially because requiring students to take survey courses that no professor wants to teach will often mean that students have trouble finding places in the required courses, sometimes delaying their graduation. The pork barrel principle is now applied to most requirements for undergraduate general education, undergraduate departmental majors, and graduate degree programs.

Meant to serve the interests of professors, the pork barrel principle serves most students badly. For example, undergraduates majoring in physics or biology find themselves unable to take a general survey course in an unfamiliar subject like Greek and Roman literature or classical music and must settle for a specialized course, perhaps on Greek women or black jazz, that they are unprepared to take and cannot put into context. Undergraduate English majors interested mainly in nineteenth-century novels are unable to take additional courses on other sorts of English literature or on French or Russian novels, but must instead satisfy arbitrary requirements with courses on popular culture, feminist films, or third-world literature. Graduate students in history specializing in French colonies in Africa are unable to take courses on economics, France, or French because they must satisfy arbitrary requirements with seminars on the history of Latin America, China, or Oceania. As a result, instead of acquiring a broad general education or a command of a broad segment of their chosen field, students take a ragbag of largely unrelated courses. Not just undergraduate majors but also graduate students acquire only a narrow familiarity with their specialty, with a smattering of other specialized knowledge that contributes little or nothing to their main subject. The graduate students may broaden their training by serving as teaching assistants in an undergraduate survey course, but they seldom gain much breadth by writing their doctoral dissertations, which are usually very specialized.

This much may seem to support critics who think that research undermines teaching. But such critics, though they may know what professors who do specialized and fashionable research are like, ignore what professors who do little or no research are like. Most of the latter, who remain a substantial majority at less prestigious institutions and a substantial minority at more prestigious ones, are the true deadwood of American academics. Most are mediocre teachers, who spend little time on their courses and repeat the same lectures from the same notes for years. As Jencks and Riesman put it some time ago,

> Teachers cannot remain stimulating unless they also continue to learn, and while this learning may not focus on small, manageable "research problems," it is research by any reasonable definition. When a teacher stops doing it, he begins to repeat himself and eventually loses touch

with both the young and the world around him. Research in this general sense does not, of course, necessarily lead to publication, but that is its most common result. Publication is the only way a man can communicate with a significant number of colleagues or other adults. Those who do not publish usually feel they have not learned anything worth communicating to adults. This means they have not learned much worth communicating to the young either.[16]

In other words, being a good teacher requires knowing one's subject well, having an active interest in it, and staying involved in it. Except for a few professors who suffer from writer's block, this means writing on their subject, though not always publishing a great deal.

Most studies of the relationship between teaching and research should be suspect, because they almost always measure teaching by student evaluations, which as we have seen are unreliable, while measuring research by numbers of publications, regardless of content or quality. Nevertheless, as a Byzantinist used to dealing with inadequate evidence, I am ready to look at such studies as we have. According to Derek Bok, "the most comprehensive treatment of this subject" is a 1987 article by Kenneth Feldman, who summarized thirty heterogeneous studies of varied samples at a range of dates.[17] Feldman found that "research productivity is positively but very weakly correlated with overall teaching effectiveness (as assessed by students)." But this overall finding masks some important differences in the qualities evaluated. Much the strongest correlations were positive ones between scholarly productivity and (in order) (1) the "teacher's knowledge of the subject"; (2) the "preparation [and] organization of the course"; (3) the "clarity of course objectives and requirements"; and (4) the "teacher's intellectual expansiveness (and intelligence)." By contrast, scholarly productivity showed (statistically insignificant) negative correlations between scholarly productivity and just three qualities: (1) the "instructor's fairness; impartiality of evaluation of students; [and] quality of examinations"; (2) the "teacher's encouragement of questions and discussion, and openness to opinions of others"; and (3) the "teacher's availability and helpfulness."[18]

Note that all four of the strongest correlations are with the most important features of any good course, especially the professor's knowledge of the subject but also his preparation, organization, clarity, and intellectual distinction. On the other hand, all three of the marginally negative correlations correspond to the sort of complaints that poor students often make when they get bad grades: the professor was unfair or biased, the examination was too hard, the professor preferred his informed views to their uninformed ones, and the professor refused to grant extensions or to raise low grades. After all, students who get As very seldom complain that the professor has graded them unfairly, that the examination was too hard, or that the professor refused to raise their grade. Of course such complaints can also be legitimate; the professor could indeed be unfair or biased, or not open to valid ideas other than his own, or unresponsive to the real educational needs of his students. Such complaints are particularly likely to be justified in the case of highly ideological professors, many of whom do research of their own sort. Nonetheless, all things being equal, even as measured by the badly flawed instrument of student course evaluations, the best courses appear to be offered by professors who do considerable amounts of research. Feldman found no basis for the idea that research distracts professors from good teaching.

Most of the preceding discussion concerns lectures, which even professors who know very little about their subject can prepare the night before class from a few textbooks or reference works (or just one). By contrast, those with limited knowledge of the subject find it much harder to prepare discussions, seminars, and tutorials. Discussions, seminars, and tutorials require the professor to react spontaneously to students' ideas, which in seminars and tutorials take the form of reports and papers drawn from sources that the professor may not know well. The professor who knows his field thoroughly from his research may scarcely need to prepare for specific seminars and tutorials, because his research itself was the best preparation for them.[19] But professors who have done little research will either need to spend long hours learning whatever is likely to come up in class or do a poor job of conducting the discussion, tutorial, or seminar. If well conducted, however, discussions, tutorials, and seminars are often better ways of teaching than lectures, above all because they involve the students more and force them to pay more attention to the subject. Though professors can fool some of their students some of the time, especially by witty banter that avoids the subject, as a rule the more the professor knows about the material, the better the discussion, tutorial, or seminar will be.

Many people think that a professor's teaching skills are more important than his knowing the subject he teaches because they remember their favorite teachers from grade school. Since practically all elementary school teachers have a basic knowledge of reading, writing, and arithmetic, the best teachers of these subjects are skilled in teaching students who are unfamiliar with school and learning. But imagine an elementary school teacher (and I suspect some exist) who was *not* able to read, write, or do arithmetic adequately. How much would it matter if his students loved him, enjoyed his teaching techniques, found his classes wonderful, much preferred them to the classes taught by literate teachers, and organized protests with their parents if he was fired? The students might remember this charismatic teacher fondly all their lives, but they also might find themselves at a lifelong disadvantage because they had been given inadequate grounding in reading, writing, or arithmetic at the beginning of their education. Except for some students who need remedial classes, most of whom should not even be in college until they have taken those classes, college students already have basic learning skills. What they need to learn is the subject of their courses, as only someone who knows it well can teach it to them.

If you still think that whether students like a professor is more important than whether he knows his subject, consider a few comparisons. Should you choose a doctor who has a pleasant personality and never prescribes unpleasant or difficult treatments even if he leaves your medical problems undiagnosed and untreated? Should you choose a financial adviser who has a pleasant personality and reassures you about your financial situation even if he knows little about investments and consistently loses you money? What about a lawyer with a pleasant and reassuring manner who knows little about the law and loses your case through incompetence? The many people who do choose doctors, brokers, and lawyers for such reasons usually come to regret it. Though college students who choose their professors on a similar basis seem to have fewer regrets, the reason is probably that they seldom think about their education at all and, if they get good grades, see no signs of failure as clearly as the patient who remains ill, the investor who loses his money, or the client who loses his case. Besides, most students are having their tuition paid by their parents, by scholarships, or by student loans that will need to be repaid only in an indefinite future that they never think about. In the meantime, college life can be more fun without reading books, writing papers, or going to class.

It should be obvious that a professor who knows his subject thoroughly and has published extensively on it is much more likely to teach it well than a professor with a weak grasp of his subject who has never published on it. The latter sort of professor may still get good teaching evaluations for being an easy grader (because if you mark everything right you can do without knowing what actually is right), open to student ideas (because you can be ready to consider any possibility if you have no idea what is right), and available to chat all day about sports (because if you do no research you have lots of free time). But none of those things makes you a good teacher. Although most students are poorly qualified to tell whether a professor knows his subject, by the end of the semester the smartest ones should be able to tell the difference between a real expert and someone unable to answer elementary questions coherently. Ignorant professors usually lack the acting skills of "Dr. Fox," and even he might have been found out during a full term of classes.

Some students can also tell when a professor is seriously biased, though others will think he has supplied the only defensible interpretation and his opponents' views are simply the result of racism, sexism, "positivism" (the favorite derogatory term for not being a postmodernist), or other sorts of supposed prejudice or error. Perhaps the problem that students are most likely to overlook is that taking a series of overspecialized and unrelated courses, no matter how well they are taught individually, results in an unbalanced, incoherent, and incomplete education. Yet biased or overspecialized teaching need not result from doing research as such, though it may result from doing overly specialized or ideological research. Just as not all teaching is good teaching, even if students give it good ratings, not all research is good research, even if it is published. The next chapter will consider what good scholarship is, along with the related issue of professorial tenure.

Chapter 5

WHAT IS GOOD RESEARCH?

The Issue of Tenure

Abolishing tenure is often proposed as a solution to the problems of universities, but I have never heard a convincing explanation of how it would actually help solve any of those problems. Most people who propose it are either university administrators or outsiders with little understanding of universities. Any administrator who wants to abolish tenure should answer these five questions:

1. Have you monitored all new job searches in the departments under you and vetoed any job offers to candidates who were recommended by those departments?
2. Have you monitored all new tenure decisions under you and denied tenure to any candidates who were recommended by their departments?
3. Have you repeatedly given any tenured professors no annual salary increase at all because of poor performance (not because of a general salary freeze)?
4. Have you increased the teaching loads of any tenured professors because they have done little or no research?
5. Have you abolished any entire department or academic program because it was performing poorly or had become obsolete?

Scarcely any administrators could truthfully answer yes to all five of these questions, and very few could truthfully answer yes to even one of them. Yet if administrators do none of these things, none of which requires changes to the present tenure system, why should we believe that if tenure were abolished the same administrators would be more careful in monitoring the performance of their professors? Why should we not think instead that these administrators would use their new power to intimidate or dismiss professors who criticized the administration, annoyed their colleagues, or attracted unfavorable attention by their opinions?

If the problem is that we have too many mediocre professors—as I think we do—abolishing tenure would be very unlikely to help and would probably make things even worse. The right way to solve the problem of mediocre professors is to hire good professors in the first place—not to hire mediocre ones, fire them, and replace them with other mediocre professors in rotation. Naturally even conscientious efforts to hire good professors can result in occasional mistakes, but serious mistakes should become apparent during the five years before an assistant professor comes up for tenure, and in those cases tenure should be denied. Truly incompetent or dishonest professors can and should be fired even if they have tenure. If despite rigorous hiring and tenure procedures a few professors turn out to be clearly substandard, they should receive no raises for years and should have their teaching loads increased, which will keep them from being too expensive and may even induce them to leave or retire voluntarily (or conceivably to reform). If they do little or no research despite light teaching loads that were meant to give them time for research, they should have their teaching loads increased and then be given or denied raises on the basis of their teaching.

In evaluating research, administrators should be careful (as many of them are not) to be fair to professors who publish less while working on a long-term research project that may turn out to be much more valuable than frequent but insignificant publications. A reasonable approach would be to reward publication as it occurs but to give a large raise to a professor who publishes a major book or article summarizing a project representing the work of a number of years. Admittedly, some professors excuse their lack of publications by claiming to be working on a long-term project that is more or less a sham and will never be completed. To deal with this possibility, their supervisors should periodically ask experts from outside the university to evaluate the work in progress on the basis of notes and incomplete drafts. A favorable report may not justify a large raise but should justify retaining a teaching load with time to continue the research. An unfavorable report should result in an increased teaching load. As for obsolete or poorly performing departments or programs, which do exist, they should be abolished along with the tenure of their professors, though any professors worth keeping should be transferred to other departments or programs.

The faculty may well oppose an administration that abolishes academic programs and overrides departmental recommendations on hiring and tenure, but if each case is properly documented and defended, the faculty will object far less than they would to the abolition of tenure itself. Any critics of tenure who think that monitoring hiring, tenure decisions, and academic programs is too much work to expect of administrators with more important things to do should explain why administrators would monitor hiring, professors' performance, and academic programs any better if tenure were abolished. (Such critics should also acknowledge their own assumption that monitoring the quality of professors is not worth an administrator's time and should then explain why abolishing tenure is important if the quality of professors is unimportant.) Of course, without any monitoring of most professors, administrators will still learn about those who criticize the administration or are themselves criticized, including whistle-blowers and people with unconventional opinions, particularly conservative ones (which are not just unusual but highly controversial at almost all universities). Whistle-blowers, mavericks, and conservatives are the professors whom abolishing tenure would endanger most.

While some people outside universities may instinctively sympathize with administrators rather than faculty, such sympathies are misplaced from almost any point of view, whether managerial or academic, conservative or liberal. Abuses of power by academic administrators have been extensively documented at many universities.[1] My own distrust of administrators has been influenced by my experience with three very different institutions: Hillsdale College, Saint Louis University, and Harvard University. When I arrived both Hillsdale and SLU had

presidents, George Roche III and Fr. Lawrence Biondi, who treated their
faculty with contempt and regarded tenure as a nuisance. Yet Roche was
president of Hillsdale for twenty-eight years and Biondi was president of
SLU for twenty-six years; by the time I came, the overwhelming majority of their professors had been hired under their authority. If most of
those professors were mediocre—and they were—Roche and Biondi
were ultimately responsible. Neither of them had any real interest in
scholarship or education.

Both Roche and Biondi were mainly interested in public relations
and especially in building buildings, most of which were expensive, ugly,
and poorly suited to education. Their favorite professors were mediocre
sycophants, and the professors they disliked most were their own critics, who were often the best professors. Both presidents liked to have
subordinates threaten their critics with lawsuits, and both declared that
academic freedom had consequences, meaning that professors were
free to criticize the administration but would suffer if they did. (If this
is freedom, most dictatorships are free.) In the final act of his administration, which led to his speedy departure, Biondi gave almost identical
raises to almost all his faculty—good, bad, or indifferent—and used his
power over salaries only to penalize a few critics, whom he denounced
publicly.[2] He had already forced out a charismatic young Jesuit professor
as "detrimental to the mission of the university," partly for being a critic
and partly for being a conservative.

My experience with the Harvard administration is more compli-
cated. As a Harvard PhD in 1977 I took a prominent part in publiciz-
ing the administration's plan largely to dismantle Dumbarton Oaks
(DO), a research institute in Washington that included a center for
Byzantine studies where I held a fellowship. The unfavorable publicity
forced Harvard to abandon its plan, though it soon managed to abolish
the Byzantine center and its faculty and to siphon off much of DO's
endowment anyway.[3] Since then I have learned from various places
where I applied for jobs that they had received negative reports about
me from DO.[4] I have applied for further fellowships from DO five times
and been rejected each time, though for the same research I have won
more competitive fellowships. Before 1977 I had a book accepted in
the series of Dumbarton Oaks Studies and two articles accepted in the
annual *Dumbarton Oaks Papers*; since then, the two articles I submitted

have been rejected, though one was then published by a more selective journal and the other as a book. I have applied for tenure-track jobs that DO has subsidized at four different universities and been rejected each time. I reached the interview stage at just one, the University of Minnesota, where three different professors told me that after their department voted unanimously to hire me, DO forced them to back down by threatening to withdraw its funding if I were hired. This looks very much like retaliation by administrators against a critic on grounds unrelated to academic merit. If Harvard administrators act this way, what administrators can be trusted?

In fact, abolishing tenure would probably lead to dismissing even fewer professors than at present. At least some professors are denied tenure now, often because they fail to meet specified requirements in ways that are hard to overlook; the most common reason is failure to publish a book by the sixth year of employment. Were there no tenure review, such professors might well be continued indefinitely from year to year, always insisting that they needed just a little more time in order to publish, or arguing that since many senior professors had published nothing for years without being dismissed, why should junior professors be dismissed for the same reason? Most departments would probably resist any dismissals at all, because once the worst or most controversial professor in the department had been fired, the next worst or most controversial would be endangered, and then the next, so that almost everyone could eventually be at risk.

As it is, many departments deliberately hire weak candidates to make their current professors look better. But if tenure were abolished, the incentives to hire weak candidates would become far stronger, because the danger of hiring better ones would be that the department's other professors might be fired, rather than just be given lower raises or made to look inferior. Most professors and administrators might, however, be happy to dismiss a conservative professor for being insufficiently committed to "diversity," "inclusiveness," or another currently fashionable form of "social justice." Some might also favor firing an outstanding professor on grounds of "elitism," which means he has high standards, or "lack of collegiality," which means his colleagues dislike or envy him. (Some professors are denied tenure now for both sorts of reasons.) Without tenure or the prospect of it, many of the best professors, and even more of the few conservative professors, would leave a profession that in most respects is already insecure, unrewarding, and hostile to both conservatism and achievement. I myself would probably have left.

Abolishing tenure would result not in wholesale dismissals of bad professors but in a major transfer of power from faculty to administrators, who do less work than professors, are far better paid, and are already busy shifting resources away from instruction to administration, construction of buildings, leftist indoctrination, and other expenditures that contribute little or nothing to education. The ideal of shared governance of universities, in which the faculty plays a role along with the administration, would become meaningless or dysfunctional if the faculty had to try to govern while constantly worrying about losing their jobs. Academic freedom, already seriously compromised for anyone outside the current consensus of opinion in universities, would suffer even more. Under such circumstances, most professors who remained could be expected to put their job security ahead of anything else, certainly well ahead of hiring colleagues better than themselves, something that they are already very reluctant to do. Since, as we have seen, a reputation as a good teacher is easy to acquire through easy assignments and lenient grading, in practice not hiring colleagues better than oneself means not hiring candidates with a better reputation for doing research.

Types of Academic Research

This brings us to the question of what good research is and whether a reputation for being a good scholar means anything more than a reputation for being a good teacher. A reputation as a good scholar is certainly harder to get. Most professors, like most students, find that researching and writing anything original and substantial is hard work, especially without the incentives of requirements and deadlines. For this reason most professors never research and write much more than their dissertation, which they later turn into a book. In the process they add some research and writing, impelled by applying for jobs or for tenure, but they seldom do as much scholarly work again as they did for the original dissertation. Even if after getting tenure they write more articles or a second book on the general subject of their dissertation, most of them never come up with a second major research project (if indeed they came up with their dissertation topic, rather than having it assigned to them by their adviser). The capacity to develop a new and different research project after the dissertation is in fact a key test of scholarly curiosity and breadth. Admittedly, if the dissertation makes a truly significant contribution to scholarship, that is itself evidence of scholarly ability. Yet in America today, few dissertations pass that test, and undistinguished dissertations seldom lead to distinguished books or distinguished articles.

Besides books based on dissertations, professors today produce quite a lot of "research" that contributes little or nothing to scholarship. Perhaps the most common examples of such undistinguished research are delivered as papers at scholarly conferences. This is true despite the fact that in principle scholarly conferences should be useful or even necessary, and some actually do perform important functions. Specialists in any field, who usually teach at different universities far away from each other, can benefit from seeing each other regularly at a general conference or convention, where they can find out about each other's research during the months or years before it can be finished, published, and circulated. Moreover, some conferences devoted to a specific topic (perhaps better termed "workshops" or "colloquia" than conferences) bring together specialists whose papers can advance scholarly knowledge by putting together complementary or contrasting discoveries. In practice, however, most conferences of both types are largely a waste of time and money—or worse, because without exchanging real ideas or real discoveries they spread and reinforce scholarly fads and distract scholars who could be doing original research instead of preparing unoriginal conference papers.

Most general conference papers convey nothing important, as should be obvious from the large numbers of very short papers (sometimes five minutes) and even "posters" or "papers read by title" that are never read aloud at all. Most conferences accept practically all submissions. Papers that have little to do with each other are often grouped into sessions with vague or misleadingly specific titles, sometimes presided over by a commentator who tries to pretend that they have something in common. Many colloquia and workshops also have vague or misleadingly specific titles and bring together essentially unrelated papers. In an attempt to avoid this problem, certain colloquia and workshops consist of papers with set topics assigned to specific specialists; but these often result in a series of short papers that simply summarize what has previously been published. After attending dozens of conferences, I now attend them very selectively, having found that most of the papers are merely meant to pad the credentials of the participants and give them an excuse to travel and see their friends. The organizers go to a good deal of trouble setting up the conferences but are rewarded by their university administrators, who consider hosting a conference a sign of prestige, and by their colleagues, who often invite them back. Certainly we should have some academic conferences, but they would be more useful if they were fewer and smaller, because opportunities to deliver papers now far exceed the number of papers worth hearing.

While just delivering a paper at a conference is an academic credential for young scholars seeking jobs and professors submitting annual activity reports, many conferences, especially workshops and colloquia, also lead to published collections of the papers, which are edited by the organizers. For some reason publishers like such collections, even if they include papers that few journals would consider original or important enough to publish as articles. Many scholars consequently publish scarcely anything but conference papers. I myself have published seven. Years ago, when I was a postdoctoral fellow at Stanford trying to get a tenure-track job, I organized a faculty seminar whose papers were later published by Stanford University Press. Taking a subject I thought needed exploring ("Renaissances Before the Renaissance: Cultural Revivals of Late Antiquity and the Middle Ages"), I chose six topics and six speakers and received a grant to fly in several fine scholars. The papers were long enough to say something significant, since they were delivered as hour-long lectures to an audience of Stanford faculty and graduate students, and I wrote an introduction and conclusion to tie the book together. The book has its merits, but I have never been tempted to try such a thing again. The main problem is that multiple authorship, without drastic editing or a series of unlikely coincidences, cannot produce a truly coherent book. And if it cannot, why not just have scholars publish separate journal articles on topics that they choose themselves because they have something new and important to say about them?

A related phenomenon is the collective volume not based on a conference, whether an encyclopedia, dictionary, handbook, or collaborative textbook. For such books the editor assembles contributors and assigns topics. These collective volumes tend to be somewhat more useful than conference volumes. We all need reference works that are better than Wikipedia (which is usually much too superficial and unreliable for scholarly purposes). Collaborating on encyclopedias, dictionaries, and handbooks is practically inevitable anyway, because no single scholar can be an expert on everything that they should contain and no intelligent reader expects such a book to have a uniform point of view. Collaborating on a textbook is more problematic, because even with the usual introduction by the editor the book cannot give a unified view of its subject; but this may not be a serious problem if the book is mainly used as a reference work or as a textbook in a course where the professor provides the overall point of view. Publishers also like these books, because many libraries think they need to buy them and the contributors can be paid little or nothing; after all, they want to increase the number of their publications and know that their contributions are almost certain to be accepted. I contributed to five collective volumes before deciding to stop accepting such invitations.[5] As with conferences and conference volumes, these collaborations have become much too common. Most are of uneven or poor quality, and they distract scholars from doing original research, which these works accommodate only rarely and with difficulty.

Popularizations and basic textbooks by single authors are another form of publication that sounds better in theory than it usually is in practice. In principle, scholars should try to make research in their field accessible to undergraduates and a wider educated readership. Though some good popularizations and basic textbooks are published, most of them, even those by scholars, are superficial and full of errors and oversimplifications. Most publishers and authors of popularizations, and most purveyors of popularizations like bookstores and book clubs, seem to assume, rightly or wrongly, that their readers want simplistic scholarship, overblown generalizations, and imaginary vignettes, with no subtleties, qualifications, or footnotes. My one popularizing book, which is sometimes used as a textbook, is a short history of Byzantium based on an earlier history of mine that was about four times as long. The shorter history was harder to write than I had expected, because I was always struggling to simplify without distorting and seldom had the pleasure of learning something new myself, which is what makes research most rewarding for a scholar. Including translations into French, German, Spanish, Italian, Greek, Chinese, Romanian, and Korean, the book has earned me about $10,000, a sum I could have earned much more quickly and easily by teaching an extra class in the summer. In any case, even the best popularizations and basic textbooks hardly ever contribute to scholarship. Perhaps universities should reward professors for such books under the category of teaching or service, not research.

On the other hand, a comprehensive survey by a single author, which may be usable as a textbook and should be accessible to a wider audience, can make a real contribution to scholarship. In the increasingly specialized and fragmented world of academic writing, some scholars need to put specialized literature into context in an effort to resolve or correct its inevitable disagreements, inconsistencies, and mistakes, and to draw the kind of general conclusions that specialized monographs cannot. In practice, however, this form of academic writing has become rare, as specialization has taken over. Most surveys are either collaborations or popularizations, and even most handbooks by a single author just compile and summarize the views of different specialists. Though Marxists, postmodernists, and other ideologues sometimes write surveys that put specialized work into context and arrive at general conclusions, their views are usually too selective and distorted to satisfy anyone but their fellow ideologues. I have undertaken two comprehensive surveys, one of Byzantine history and another of the Byzantine historians (in three parts, with the third still in progress). These have met not so much with criticism as with bafflement. My colleagues, apparently expecting handbooks that would simply summarize earlier views, seemed surprised to find me suggesting original interpretations and rejecting many views of previous specialists and ideologues. Most scholars now see no place in scholarship for comprehensive studies—which means that most scholars have given up the attempt to see their subject as a whole.

The largest single category of today's academic publications, and the overwhelming preponderance of today's original research, is specialized monographs and journal articles. A great many of these, probably the majority, are based on dissertations, including articles derived from dissertations, first books revised from dissertations, and second books that expand upon first books revised from dissertations. (Hollywood would call them remakes, sequels, or spinoffs.) This is especially unfortunate because few dissertations make major advances in scholarship. As Christopher Jencks and David Riesman observed almost fifty years ago,

> Everyone...bewails the standard doctoral dissertation, constructed with scissors, paste, five or ten pounds of 3x5 cards [now with equivalent computer files], a few hundred obliquely relevant citations, and (in some fields) a few hundred tests of statistical significance. This sort of exercise is usually attacked as irrelevant for future teachers and defended as appropriate for future scholars. In most cases, however, it is irrelevant for anyone, no matter what his plans.[6]

Since those words were written, such dissertations have only become more common. A more recent critic has observed,

> If you survey dissertation topics in any humanistic field, it's hard not to be struck by the conformity of the topics. There is a lemminglike quality to the intellectual product that graduate students produce. The overwhelming majority of American history doctoral studies today are on social history and "new" history, with emphasis on postmodernism and all of its many cousins.[7]

The same critic supplies the explanation: "Graduate students see the current trend. They see the absolute scarcity of jobs, and they see what type of work is rewarded, with jobs and publications, and what type is not."[8] In other words, the present academic job market is actively discouraging good dissertations and encouraging certain kinds of mediocre or bad dissertations. Mediocre or bad dissertations have therefore become not just the main credentials for most academic careers but the foundation of most academic research and publications.

How Research Is Judged Now

Only the most doctrinaire postmodernist would maintain that there is no difference between good, mediocre, and bad research, or that there can be no way to tell the difference. In the case of dissertations, however, scarcely anyone now tries to determine the difference, because scarcely anyone reads dissertations in their original form. The person most likely to read a dissertation is the dissertation director, who after commenting on it privately to its author evaluates it only by accepting it, as he almost always does after revisions, and by describing it briefly in his letters of recommendation for his student, often before the student finishes it. After reading well over 2,000 letters of recommendation for academic job applicants, I cannot recall seeing a single letter that even hinted that the dissertation was mediocre or (in the case of dissertations in progress) was expected to be mediocre. The majority of letters praised the dissertation to the skies. (A few letters, never written by the actual dissertation director, admitted that the recommender had not read the dissertation or lacked the expertise to judge it adequately.) Some dissertations must surely deserve praise, but how can we tell which ones? Given the importance of dissertations as credentials on the job market and as the basis of future publications, this is a vital part of the larger question of how we should judge academic research and publications.

To begin with, the usual assumption has long been that published books and articles are better than work that has not been accepted for publication. Everyone acknowledges exceptions to this rule. Some journals are known to be less selective than others, and a few, especially online journals, accept almost every article submitted to them, so that publication there means little or nothing. For books, some presses also accept nearly everything submitted to them, including vanity presses and certain others, like the Edwin Mellen Press and University Press of America. Admittedly, the days are gone when the most prestigious university presses like Oxford, Cambridge, and Harvard published only important scholarly books; even those presses now make money by publishing some popularizations that make no real contribution to scholarship. Some leading commercial presses, like Routledge and Palgrave Macmillan, also publish both popularizations and scholarly studies. Popularizations are however easy to identify, and most books published by reputable presses that are not popularizations are reputable scholarly studies. Although the same is not necessarily true of scholarly studies published by the less prestigious university presses, the books they accept are usually better than the books they reject. While major presses will not publish some specialized monographs because their sales will not cover their costs, a number of selective monograph series publish the best of these monographs, though sometimes in a cheap format sold at a high price.

A majority of scholars, including me, think that almost all serious scholarship can still be published somewhere. Some dissenters claim that opportunities for scholarly publication are too limited, because the number of books and articles that young scholars need to have published in order to get jobs and tenure is greater than the number of books and articles published by respectable presses and journals.[9] While this calculation is doubtless correct, it should be a problem only on the extremely implausible assumption that even the worst young scholars deserve to be hired and given tenure, or on the more plausible assumption that inferior publications are crowding out scholarly work that deserves to be published. For the latter assumption my own experience should not be a bad test. I have powerful ideological and institutional enemies, have never held a permanent position at a prestigious university, write on the unfashionable subject of Byzantine history and literature, and openly reject postmodernism, Marxism, gender theory, and other currently fashionable ideologies. Yet everything I wanted published has eventually appeared in print, including two specialized monographs in monograph series distributed by Harvard and Columbia University Presses, four books published by Stanford University Press, and three books published by Palgrave Macmillan. If you are skeptical about the quality of my work, you should be that much less skeptical of my belief that publishing academic research is not impossibly difficult.

This is not to say that my publications have encountered no obstacles. A sympathetic Oxford professor once warned me not to submit anything to Oxford University Press, because my enemies would block its acceptance. Suspicions of similar situations at Harvard University Press and the University of California Press have led me not to submit anything to them. When Palgrave Macmillan (then just Macmillan) asked me to write a short history of Byzantium, my preliminary outline received a reader's report so intemperate that the editor sent me a contract anyway. Perhaps more worrisome is the trouble that my wife and I have had in publishing two controversial articles, one jointly authored. Our joint article, which interpreted the mosaics at Ravenna of the emperor Justinian (527–65) and his empress Theodora on the basis of history and archeology rather than fashionable theorizing, appeared in the *Art*

Bulletin after its editor rejected a negative reader's report and predicted (mistakenly) that it would be widely criticized.[10] The other article, which argued that the Western emperor Gratian chose the Eastern emperor Theodosius I (379–95) because of a prophecy that the next Eastern emperor's name would begin with THEOD, was rejected three times before being accepted by an Italian journal on the recommendation of a senior Roman historian, Sir Fergus Millar.[11] By combining political and cultural history, that article seems to have broken a tacit agreement between traditionalists and postmodernists to ignore each other's work, a taboo that has given certain classicists similar trouble.[12] Yet even these articles were finally published.

Many of us think the main problem with academic publications today is that too many of them are of poor quality, or at least have nothing important to say. The Dr. Fox lecture that exposed bad teaching found its counterpart for academic publication in an article published in 1996 by the left-wing physicist Alan Sokal in the postmodernist journal *Social Text*, entitled "Transgressing the Boundaries: Towards a Transformative Hermeneutics of Quantum Gravity." The article began by dismissing "the dogma imposed by the long post-Enlightenment hegemony over the Western intellectual outlook, which can be summarized briefly as follows: that there exists an external world, whose properties are independent of any individual human being and indeed of humanity as a whole," continuing with similar postmodernist and pseudoscientific claptrap. The author intended this article, as he explained in a second article that *Social Text* rejected, as "a parody . . . a mélange of truths, half-truths, quarter-truths, falsehoods, non sequiturs, and syntactically correct sentences that have no meaning whatsoever."[13]

After gaining a good deal of publicity and causing some temporary discomfiture to some postmodernists, this article ultimately changed nothing in academic publishing. While Sokal could demonstrate that the scientific content of his article included many outright errors and self-contradictions, it seems to have been no worse than many other highly acclaimed postmodernist publications in the humanities and social sciences, though their fallacies may have been harder to refute. Even in the natural sciences, extremely bad work can be published. In 1998 the editor of the *British Medical Journal* sent 200 of her regular reviewers an article that included eight deliberate conceptual errors; nobody caught them all, and the average number of errors detected was under two. More recently, the Harvard biologist John Bohannon wrote an article deliberately concocted to be worthless on the treatment of cancer and submitted it under an assumed name to 304 peer-reviewed science journals; it was accepted by 157 and rejected by just 98.[14] In no field can acceptance for publication be taken as proof of scholarly excellence.

One popular idea for distinguishing which publications are important is to keep track of how often other publications cite them. One might think that computing such citations would at least screen out publications that have nothing new or important to say. Yet what the number of citations primarily shows is a publication's fashionability, which as matters stand is probably the main reason for the publication of bad books and articles. Frequently cited publications often include nothing new and are cited merely because they agree with the scholarly orthodoxy accepted by the authors who cite them. Conversely, fewer citations can be expected of books and articles that treat unfashionable subjects using unfashionable approaches—that is, that treat neglected subjects using new and original methods. (Remarkably, in the humanities today the word "innovative" is largely reserved for stale adaptations of ideas first expressed more than forty years ago by Michel Foucault, Jacques Derrida, Paul de Man, and other postmodernists.) Besides, many citations in publications are of handbooks and surveys that add nothing of their own but simply summarize earlier publications. Such citations are often justified—because the alternative is to include long footnotes that cite the earlier publications one by one—but this need not mean that the compilers of the latest bibliographical survey are major scholars in their own right. Citation indexes by themselves say little about a publication's originality or value.

In theory, the best guide to the value of a book or article should be the readers' reports solicited by editors of journals and presses and, in the case of books, published book reviews. Excerpts from favorable readers' reports often appear (with the readers' permission) as blurbs on the cover of the published book. In practice, reviewers have strong incentives to judge their colleagues' work more favorably than it deserves, unless those colleagues strongly disagree with the reviewers' own work or are personal enemies. Readers' reports are supposed to be anonymous, and for articles are often "double-blind," so that the authors are not supposed to know who the readers are and the readers are not supposed to know who the authors are. In most fields, however, specialists are few enough that experienced scholars can often make a good guess about the author's identity from an article or a good guess about the reviewer's identity from a reader's report. (The main exceptions are graduate students and recent PhDs, whose scholarly profiles are still unfamiliar to other scholars.) Published book reviews are hardly ever anonymous and seldom unfavorable, because negative reviews make enemies. Most reviews follow a predictable format, making a few minor criticisms and corrections (to show that the reviewer knows the subject) but concluding that the book is nonetheless extremely valuable.

One of the few advantages of not being a postmodernist, Marxist, or feminist is that I can review most books more or less candidly and objectively. Out of 78 books on which I have published reviews so far, by my count I gave 24 books mostly favorable reviews, 26 books mostly unfavorable reviews, and 28 books (largely collaborative volumes) mixed reviews. The average quality of the books and articles submitted for publication that I reviewed for presses and journals was actually rather similar to the average quality of the published books I reviewed.[15] Among the books I gave favorable or mixed reviews, or recommended for publication, were some that failed to convince me by their arguments but were cogent and intelligent enough that I thought they deserved a hearing. Of course I have also read many other books and articles in the course of my research or out of scholarly interest. While my sample is far from scientific, my overall impression is that roughly half the books and articles published today are not worth publishing, though a few of those might have been brought up to minimal standards with extensive revisions. This impression is based on reasonably wide reading within the general field of ancient and medieval history and literature, though obviously the proportions of deserving books that are published may be different in other fields. The proportions would however need to be radically different to alter my conclusion that most deserving books can be published and that many undeserving books are published too.

My reading includes the books that I read between 2003 and 2006 as one of three members of the selection committee for the American Historical Association's Breasted Prize for the best history before AD 1000. One member of this committee is replaced every year, and the longest-serving member serves as chair. During my first two years the committee came to consensus decisions of which I approved. During my third year, when I was chair, the newest member of the committee announced that because he was moving that summer he had no time to read most of the books. However, he insisted that the prize be awarded to a fashionable survey of the early Middle Ages that rejected the bulk of the economic and demographic evidence because it conflicted with Marxist ideology.[16] The third member of the committee agreed with me that other books were better, but our colleague insisted so heatedly that the third member, who had to serve with him the next year, gave in. Faced with the chair's assigned task of writing a statement awarding the prize to a book I considered unacceptable, I resigned from the committee. This experience confirmed my skepticism about the meaning of book prizes. At best, such prizes are subject to the vicissitudes of submissions, and may be defensibly awarded to the best of a bad lot or justly denied to an excellent book not quite as good as the best one submitted. At worst, many prizes simply honor fashionable books for being fashionable. The award of the 2016 Nobel Prize in Literature to Bob Dylan, who was himself embarrassed by it, should help justify skepticism about such prizes.

Competitions for academic fellowships are different from book prizes: the fellowships are awarded not to published books but to proposals for future research that the fellowships would support. The members of the selection committees for fellowships often find themselves judging proposals far from their own fields, and tend to favor fashionable proposals submitted by professors from prestigious institutions, sometimes even if those applicants' record of past research is rather thin. One reason may be that the committees like to support supposedly promising junior scholars, but promise is notoriously hard to judge. Obviously these committees have their prejudices, which on small committees can be decisive. The best process for evaluating fellowship proposals known to me is that of the National Endowment for the Humanities (NEH), because it relies on different panels of specialists who share at least the general fields of the applicants. Most, though not all, of the NEH fellows whose work I know deserved support.[17] The NEH is now one of very few institutions making a serious effort to judge the quality of academic research—unlike, for example, the MacArthur Foundation, which now rewards fashionable and left-wing research with little regard for merit. Abolishing the NEH would do universities much more harm than good, while saving a sum that is trifling as a share of the federal budget.

Despite the deficiencies of many scholarly publications, numbers do mean something. One informed observer remarks that "more studies have than have not shown a positive relationship between the quality and quantity of academic work," noting that a "commonly cited study of physicists found the relationship between quantity of publication and quality of publication to be 0.72."[18] Journal articles, encyclopedia articles, and book chapters are often trivial and derivative; edited books and popularizations usually contribute little to scholarship; and revised and published dissertations, though better than submitted dissertations, are often mere exercises whose contribution to scholarship is minimal. Yet most of the substandard books and articles are the work of authors just going through the motions to get a job or to get tenure, and these people, who find writing hard because they have little to say, rarely publish second books that are not edited books or popularizations. Someone who has published several real books (that is, books that are not edited books or popularizations) almost always has something to say, even if it is wrong. If such authors are ideologues, at least they really believe in their ideologies, unlike most professors who write postmodernist, feminist, or Marxist boilerplate in order to win acceptance as publishing scholars without doing much work or much thinking. If a professor publishes two or more real books after finishing his dissertation, that professor is probably a real scholar, though possibly a bad one. Of course, this fairly crude test can only be applied to professors who have had time to do substantial amounts of research and writing, and are therefore usually past the stage of applying for a first job or for tenure.

How to Judge Research

How, then, can we judge scholarship more or less objectively, even near the beginning of an academic career? Some people think we cannot, but I would suggest five main criteria for scholarly excellence, which should be applicable to most kinds of scholarship, even in the natural sciences. First, the work should be new: it should say something that nobody has said before, at least in quite the same way. Second, the work should be important: it should make a significant (though perhaps small) difference in our understanding of its subject. Third, the work should be accurate: it should not be based on glaring factual errors that invalidate its conclusions. Fourth, the work should be rigorous, which is not precisely the same thing as being factually accurate: it should not be based on clear misinterpretations of the factual evidence. Fifth, the work should be intelligible, even if abstruse: at a minimum, a qualified specialist must be able to tell whether something new, important, accurate, and rigorous is buried in there somewhere. Good scholarship cannot utterly fail any of these five tests, and excellent scholarship should pass all five comfortably, if not always to the same extent.

Such criteria for scholarly excellence need to be interpreted with a degree of flexibility. Excellence in some of the five criteria can sometimes compensate for deficiencies in others. For instance, we should tolerate (but notice) errors, fallacies, or obscurities in a book that is strikingly new and important, as long as these are not so serious as to invalidate its conclusions. A new, accurate, rigorous, and intelligible point of minor but real significance can be enough to make an important article, if not perhaps an important book. A book or article can be important even if its thesis turns out to be mistaken, because it can still stimulate scholarly discussion that leads to a better explanation of an important problem. On the other hand, if the original thesis depends on clearly identifiable errors or fallacies, it will needlessly distract other scholars by forcing them to refute its errors or fallacies. For example, a book maintaining that the ancient Greeks had arrived in Greece as aliens from outer space would be new and would address an important question, the origin of the Greeks. But if the book's argument was based on obvious errors and fallacies (as it presumably would be), it would be worthless as scholarship, if not as science fiction.

Alan Sokal designed his article in *Social Text* to be of this type: it would have been new and important if it had been right, but its deliberate errors, fallacies, and obscurities made it worthless as scholarship, though an extremely useful example of the defects of postmodernism. The worst defect of postmodernism is its excessive tolerance of errors, fallacies, and obscurities, as long as they are postmodernist, "innovative," and "interesting." Note that being innovative and interesting are not among my five criteria for good scholarship. "Innovative" could be such a criterion if it meant new and original, but postmodernists tend to use it, like "interesting," merely to mean "postmodernist." "Interesting" is a hopelessly subjective concept, since very different things interest different people, and most fair-minded people will admit that they find some important subjects boring and some unimportant subjects interesting. Many scholars and students, myself included, find most postmodernist work so vacuous and self-referential as to be very tedious. This is one reason postmodernism has flourished largely unchallenged: many scholars who are interested in their fields but not in postmodernism are unwilling to pay enough attention to postmodernist work to write a systematic refutation of it, especially because if they did the postmodernists would simply deny the facts and the logic of the refutation. Having written some such refutations, I have found them a tiresome and thankless task.[19] We owe Sokal a genuine debt.

Excellent scholarship can be written by scholars who have ideological commitments, as most of us do. If these commitments are irrelevant to some or all of their scholarship, the scholars may be able to keep ideology out of their scholarship altogether. In any case, the fact that a book or article expresses ideological views need not in itself invalidate its conclusions, even if the ideology was what inspired them. A Marxist can identify clashes between social classes that really did occur. A feminist can identify women whose importance really has been neglected by scholars before feminism existed. A postmodernist can identify misleading ideas that really were devised primarily to promote the power and influence of the people who devised them. (A good case can be made that Michel Foucault invented postmodernism to promote his own power and influence.) Yet Marxists, feminists, and postmodernists—while they may be more likely than others to identify authentic class struggles, important women, and misleading ideas—are also more likely to exaggerate or imagine the existence or significance of such things. The essential criterion for evaluating ideological scholarship is that it should argue its case on the basis of facts and arguments that can also convince readers who do not share the same ideology. Such readers will not and should not be convinced by simply being told that a thesis advances the interests of women or the working class or that it agrees with the theories of Karl Marx or Michel Foucault.

These suggested criteria for judging good scholarship need to be applied not just with serious efforts at objectivity, but also by scholars with a specialized knowledge of the relevant fields. Only someone with specialized knowledge of a subject can judge reliably whether work on that subject is new, accurate, or rigorous. Something that seems new and looks accurate and rigorous to a non-specialist may be easily identified by a specialist as merely repeated from someone else's work done years before or as based on glaring factual errors or fallacious arguments. Even something that appears important to a non-specialist may be recognized by a specialist as unimportant by the standards of the field, though it may be expressed in a superficially intriguing way. Obviously, a discussion in technical language that a non-specialist will find unintelligible may be recognized by a specialist as difficult but intelligible, though perhaps expressed with unnecessary obscurity. Less obviously, technical language that sounds convincing to a non-specialist may be recognized by a specialist as a pretentious formulation of something banal, superficial, erroneous, or fallacious, or even as complete nonsense, like Sokal's parody.

Thus evaluating scholarship rigorously requires identifying the right kind of specialists and persuading them to evaluate the scholarly work in question with care and objectivity. This should be self-evident, but in today's academic world it is much too seldom done. The most serious problem is not really finding specialists who are qualified to judge, though non-specialists often do write letters of recommendation, readers' reports, evaluations for tenure and promotion, and book reviews. The main problem is that scholars have few reasons to be careful or objective and strong incentives to express judgments that are more favorable than their real opinions. A reputation for writing overly favorable recommendations or book reviews almost never hurts anyone's career. Scarcely any letters of recommendation are objective, and the rare cases when their fulsome praise is deserved are almost impossible to distinguish from the others. Readers' reports, evaluations for tenure and promotion, and book reviews all tend to be much more favorable than they ought to be, either because the writers want to avoid making an enemy, because they are teachers or friends of the person being recommended, or because they want to promote their field by helping a colleague. Even the occasional negative comment may simply reflect a personal grievance or rivalry, not a reasoned judgment. Nonetheless, as I shall suggest in the next chapter, ways can be found to extract fairly objective evaluations from qualified specialists, especially and crucially for doctoral dissertations and the job candidates who have written them.

Chapter 6

PROPOSALS FOR LEGISLATION

Two National Boards

The imbalance in the academic job market has contributed enormously to the problems with today's colleges and universities. It corrupts the whole system of hiring by overwhelming hiring committees and encouraging graduate students to write faddish and superficial dissertations in a desperate effort to attract attention. No one planned this imbalance, and scarcely anyone wanted it. The original rise in the production of doctorates to about the present level met a real demand for new professors when student enrollments soared in the sixties. When enrollments stabilized around 1970 and the demand for new professors fell markedly, the production of doctorates failed to fall nearly as much as it should have. Few people expected the crisis to remain so severe for so long. Many predicted that it would end when a wave of professors retired in the eighties and nineties, but this prediction turned out to be too optimistic, mostly because administrators chose to hire cheaper adjunct professors instead of regular professors. Although by now everyone can see that the problem will not go away by itself, the ways in which universities have adapted to it have become widely established and accepted—except by unemployed and embittered PhDs, who have little power or influence to bring about a change.

The obvious solution is to limit the number of PhDs to roughly the number of the available jobs. Yet after almost fifty years of a dysfunctional job market, nothing of the kind has happened, and new doctoral programs are sometimes being added. Incentives to have such programs are simply too strong. Universities and departments with doctoral programs are more prestigious and better funded than departments without them. Professors like to teach graduate students. Graduate students can be used to teach undergraduates for tuition waivers and small stipends, reducing the numbers and workloads of regular faculty and overall instructional costs. Although the reputations of departments that never found jobs for any of their doctorates might suffer if others placed all of theirs, in today's anarchic job market almost all departments have serious trouble with placement, and almost all can place a few students somewhere. Besides, for a single department to admit fewer doctoral students, as some have done, does scarcely anything to help. A uniform reduction in admissions in every doctoral program in the country might solve the problem—but who could impose such a reduction on every university, public and private, in every state? Moreover, the worst programs should presumably be cut more than the best ones or even eliminated altogether; but how many departments will admit that their programs are inferior? As for improving the quality of hiring, hardly anyone considers such a thing possible on a scale bigger than a single search by a single department. The consensus is therefore that nothing can be done.

An effective and inexpensive solution would be possible, though it would require some enlightened intervention from the federal government. The problems of an unbalanced academic job market, chaotic academic hiring, and inferior teaching and research could largely be solved by federal legislation creating a National Dissertation Review Board to evaluate new doctoral dissertations, along with a separate National Academic Honesty Board to judge claims of plagiarism or fraud in dissertations and academic publications. Congress should pass a law providing funding for these boards' staff and headquarters and requiring every university receiving federal aid—that is, practically every university—to submit to the Dissertation Review Board in electronic form every dissertation accepted for a doctorate. These boards could be attached to the Department of Education or the Library of Congress, or they could simply become independent government agencies. The amount of money needed for the two boards would be negligible in terms of the federal budget.

The Dissertation Review Board and Academic Honesty Board should each consist of a director and around twenty full-time senior members, one for each of the main academic fields represented by departments in most universities (philosophy, sociology, chemistry, and so on). Most of these members would be professors who are either retired or on extended leave from their home institutions. The Academic Honesty Board should draw up clear guidelines defining dishonesty in academic research and writing, including plagiarism, falsified experiments, and false claims about academic credentials. Academic dishonesty can be defined simply as a deliberate attempt at serious deception about an academic matter. (If an informed and impartial observer could have serious doubt that the deception was intentional or that the offense was serious, the accused should usually be given the benefit of the doubt.) The Academic Honesty Board should investigate dishonesty not only in dissertations but in published academic books and articles. It should be ready to investigate any such charges it received, as long as they were specific, documented, and not anonymous, though the board should keep names of accusers confidential. Substantiated charges of serious academic dishonesty by professors should be reported to the universities where they teach, and publicized if the professors do not resign and are not dismissed. If the board confirmed that scientific experiments had been falsified, that should be always be publicized, since it could cause physical harm.

The Dissertation Review Board, besides its director and full-time senior members, should also have several full-time junior employees in each field, selected by the senior members from well-qualified recent doctorates. To perform the actual judging of the dissertations, the board should identify a pool of senior scholars with a record of important research in each field, again including many retired professors. These specialized referees should all have published the results from at least one major research project in addition to their own dissertations. In the humanities, this would normally mean that they had published two books with reputable scholarly presses, but in the natural sciences (and a few other fields like philosophy and archeology, in which articles rather than books are the usual form of publication), a number of substantial articles could be taken as the equivalent. The referees would not need to travel because they could receive the dissertations by means of the Internet wherever they lived. For each dissertation they evaluated, they should be paid an honorarium of a few hundred dollars, comparable to honoraria paid by major presses for evaluating a book manuscript. Such a sum would recognize a valuable service rather than be a significant source of income.

The process of evaluating the dissertations should combine features of the manuscript selection processes of scholarly presses and those of the NEH and similar foundations for research fellowships. The process might work as follows. The junior employees of the Dissertation Review Board would first redact anything in the dissertations that would identify their authors or their institutions. Then, with the advice and approval of the senior member of the board for that field, copies of each dissertation would be sent to three referees with specialized knowledge of the dissertation topic who were not thanked or strongly praised or criticized in the dissertation (and not affiliated with the institution where the dissertation was accepted). These referees should include retired professors, many of whom have the time, interest, and expertise to do the job especially well. These three referees would rate the dissertations on a numerical scale. I suggest a 100-point scale, with a maximum of 20 points each for originality, importance, accuracy, rigor, and clarity.[1] The referees should explain their numerical ratings in written comments, which would usually be brief but in complex cases could be longer.

The referees should receive clear instructions. They should be reminded that their ratings would be important to the careers of all the doctorates in their field, and that an unfairly high rating for a dissertation would be as unjust to other PhDs as an unfairly low rating would be to the dissertation's author. What the numbers mean ought to be as clearly defined as possible. For example, on a 20-point scale, a 20 could be defined as "equal in quality to the best published work," a 1 as "of the lowest possible quality for an acceptable dissertation," a 10 as "superior in quality to about half of acceptable dissertations," and a 15 as "superior in quality to about three-quarters of acceptable dissertations." An unacceptable dissertation would be one that fell below the standard of an acceptable dissertation on at least one of the five criteria, or that showed evidence of plagiarism or fraud. (A dissertation plagiarized from good sources might otherwise receive high ratings on all five criteria.) If the referees differed significantly in their overall ratings, say by 5 points or more, the dissertation should be sent to two additional specialized referees. Any claims of fraud or plagiarism should be sent to the Academic Honesty Board, though if it rejected the claims, the dissertation should be sent to additional referees.

The findings of all the referees could first be discussed at a meeting of the senior board member in the relevant field with the junior employees in the same field, who would add their recommendations in disputed cases.[2] All these findings would then be forwarded to all the senior members of the board, who might meet once a month. When the referees were in substantial agreement, the board would normally make the average of their individual and cumulative ratings available online together with their comments, without attaching the names of the referees or the individual ratings. Only the names of the board members and the complete list of current referees in each field should be made available online, so that the names would not be associated with the individual comments. When the referees disagreed significantly, the board would consider their reports and normally choose the three reports that it considered most accurate to have their ratings averaged and to be made available online with their comments. Comments rejected by the board should not be made public. Substantiated claims of dishonesty would be communicated to the university that had awarded the degree, and if the university did not revoke the degree, a report outlining the dishonesty should be made available online, along with the finding that the dissertation was unacceptable. The same opportunity should be given for dissertations found unacceptable on grounds of poor quality. Efforts should be made to publish the final ratings and comments online within six months of the dissertation's submission.

No dissertation should be evaluated that was submitted before the law was passed, since this would be unfair to students who had written careless dissertations on the reasonable assumption that nobody would read them carefully. As soon as the law was passed, however, the submission of many dissertations would probably be delayed for extensive revisions. The Academic Honesty Board would be a necessary complement to the ratings; otherwise the number of plagiarized or fraudulent dissertations would probably increase because the authors knew that the quality of their work would be evaluated, as now is seldom the case. The presence of an Academic Honesty Board should however decrease the amount of academic dishonesty, because dishonest doctoral students could no longer assume that they were unlikely to be caught. No one can confidently say how much academic dishonesty occurs in dissertations now (including the falsification of scientific experiments), but no one can confidently say that it is insignificant.

Though nobody would need to pay attention to the ratings of the Dissertation Review Board, they would almost certainly attract wide interest. They would give a very good idea of how effective most departments were in preparing their doctoral students and how competitive most departments were in their hiring. The news media and guides to colleges and universities could assess and publish the ratings. Students applying to graduate school would have a good idea of the training they would receive and their job prospects afterward. As it became clear which departments were producing substandard dissertations, the number of doctoral programs and the number of PhDs should shrink, as some programs were terminated and others became more selective. Dissertations, and the supervision of dissertations, should improve. Students should feel free to write excellent and original dissertations on less fashionable topics, expecting that excellence and originality would be recognized in the ratings. Hiring should improve in most places, and wherever it did not the ratings would show which places were hiring inferior candidates. There should also be less hiring of graduate students without degrees, as departments preferred candidates whose dissertations were finished and rated. Many universities might offer one-year positions to almost all their new PhDs, replacing adjunct professors. The number of adjunct professors should decline, as those with better-rated dissertations found tenure-track jobs and others understood their prospects were bleak and left the profession. Finally, the quality of teaching and research in American universities should improve dramatically.

Possible Objections

Despite widely felt dismay at the persistent imbalance in the academic job market and the state of American universities, the proposal outlined here would inevitably draw opposition. Many professors would feel uncomfortable at being rated, even indirectly through the dissertations they supervised and the new professors they hired. Some would fear that the Academic Honesty Board might end careers because of relatively minor infractions. Some would invoke the usual arguments against hiring well-qualified candidates at low-ranking institutions ("They wouldn't be happy here."). Some would claim that the Dissertation Review Board's ratings would "privilege research over teaching" or "reduce intangible qualities to a single number" or "try to tell departments how to hire." Many administrators, secretly happy with a buyer's market in PhDs that keeps academic salaries low and professors cowed, would resist any effort to bring the market into balance. As with every attempt to improve American education at any level, the charge of "elitism" would be indignantly raised. Some leftists would see the ratings as an attack on leftism, or at any rate on postmodernism, Marxism, feminism, and other such ideologies. Some conservatives would assume that the board's ratings would be biased in favor of liberals, since most of the referees would be liberal, like most professors. Conservatives who dislike all government agencies and government spending might oppose even agencies as small and inexpensive as these. People who dislike universities might be reluctant to endorse a system that could increase their legitimacy. Others with a low opinion of government may simply assume that such a proposal is hopelessly utopian.[3]

Some of these objections are more easily addressed than others. Professors uncomfortable with being rated are unlikely to admit that they want the freedom to produce bad graduate students, to hire bad colleagues, or to publish plagiarized or fraudulent work. Yet they would have the chance to do better in the future, since past dissertations and hires would not be affected by the Dissertation Review Board. For professors who claim that their doctoral programs are currently underrated by *U.S. News* because it favors more prestigious institutions, this reform would give them a chance to be proved right: the referees, not knowing which programs produced the dissertations they rated, would not be influenced by the programs' reputations. In fact, the board's ratings would probably produce a good many surprises, as some dissertations from less prestigious programs could receive higher ratings than dissertations from more prestigious programs. The sorts of professors who think that research is a distraction from good teaching could disregard the ratings; but the argument that writing a bad or plagiarized dissertation makes one a better teacher is hard to make. If the quality of a dissertation is irrelevant to a teaching job, surely it would be better to demand not a bad or plagiarized dissertation but no dissertation—that is, no PhD. Since as it is some professors face charges of academic dishonesty evaluated by haphazard systems at their home universities in an atmosphere of controversy, surely a centralized and uniform national system would be an improvement. Though the Academic Honesty Board should be careful to avoid stigmatizing trivial lapses, most academic plagiarism and fraud is deliberate and extensive, designed to give the impression that the authors have made major contributions to scholarship when they have done nothing of the sort.

Departments could still hire anyone they chose, but most of them now require a completed or nearly completed dissertation anyway and dismiss professors who fail to earn their doctorates within a specified time. The Dissertation Review Board's ratings would be by far the best indicators of what those doctorates meant, since very few students fail graduate courses or qualifying examinations or have their completed dissertations rejected. The ratings would be much more reliable than letters of recommendation (with their formulaic praise for practically all students), or than student course evaluations (which are easily manipulated), or than conference papers (most of which are accepted automatically), or even than published articles or book chapters (many of which are evaluated carelessly). No search committee would think that the board's dissertation ratings were fully precise and reliable; but then neither are grade point averages, GRE scores, or other numbers that academics use all the time. Nobody could reasonably conclude that a dissertation with a rating of 53 was significantly worse than a dissertation with a rating of 56. The ratings would however allow search committees to look more closely at the files, whether of the best candidates, if those were what the committee wanted, or of middling candidates, if those were what the committee preferred. The board's ratings could legitimately save search committees a great deal of work.

Search committees would still be unlikely to interview a candidate with a specialty they did not need or want just because that candidate had written a dissertation with a high rating. Naturally the ratings would be no substitute for interviews and presentations on campus, which would remain the best means of identifying candidates who were good writers but poor speakers or teachers, once their basic competence had been demonstrated by the quality of their dissertations. Departments could still hire candidates on any basis they chose, including affability, fashionability, race, or sex, though they might have trouble justifying (for example) hiring a black woman with a poorly rated dissertation when a black woman with a better-rated dissertation was available in the same field. Only institutions that were seriously trying to keep or build a reputation for academic distinction would be likely to hire candidates whose dissertations had received stellar ratings in preference to those whose dissertations had received merely respectable ratings. In any case, on average the board's ratings should cause better professors to be hired than would have been hired without the ratings.

Though the board's ratings, like anything else created by human beings, would not be totally reliable, they should not be seriously distorted if they included safeguards similar to those suggested here. Despite everything that is wrong with contemporary universities, many professors retain an elementary sense of fairness, and most of them still know the difference between good and bad research.[4] This is particularly true of the mostly older and better-published professors, including retirees, who would serve as referees. The use of numerical ratings along with comments might seem arbitrary, but in fact it would promote equitable comparisons in a way that comments alone cannot do. As a wise old graduate student once remarked, "There's nothing I can do to get an enthusiastic comment from a professor who doesn't like me, but there are things I can do to make him give me an A." Those who wanted comments could still find them, both in the board's reports and in the letters of recommendation submitted for every job applicant. I can testify from many search committee meetings that professors who are so inclined can always find evidence in application files to prefer weak candidates to stronger ones, no matter how clear the evidence looks to a less partial observer. Yet professors who can argue that a fallacious and derivative article is better than an important and original book could hardly argue that a dissertation rating of 39 was better than a dissertation rating of 93. They might even have trouble arguing that their own uninformed opinion was more reliable than the opinion of three independent experts who had read the dissertation carefully. Hiring committees could ignore the evidence, but they would have trouble claiming that it meant the opposite of what it said.

The serious distortions in the present hiring process are mainly the result of the huge number of applications that must be evaluated by professors with too little time, no specialized knowledge of the subfield in which they are hiring, and incentives to hire on grounds other than merit, including likability, fashionability, ideology, race, sex, and accomplishments that might make other members of the department look worse. The professors who say that a superior researcher "wouldn't be happy here" or "wouldn't fit in here" recognize the applicant's merits and are reluctant to hire him precisely because of them. On the other hand, under a system like the one outlined here, the well-qualified referees recruited by the board would be unlikely to resent the recent doctorates they evaluated, should not know whether they were black, Hispanic, female, or likable, and should be able to see through a dissertation that merely parroted a fashionable ideology. The real question is not whether a Dissertation Review Board would produce fully reliable ratings, but whether its ratings would be better than what we have now, when virtually all positions are filled after far less careful and impartial consideration of any credentials.

If "elitism" only means excellence in education, this proposal can fairly be called "elitist." But the charge would be unfair if it implied that an undue advantage would go to whites rather than blacks or Hispanics, to men rather than women, or to graduate students from prestigious universities rather than those from less prestigious ones. Under the rating system proposed here, the referees should not know the race, sex, or university of the authors of the dissertations they rated, because they would have read the dissertations only after indications of race, sex, or university had been deleted. Since some critics would still probably charge that the system was somehow biased, those who administered it should always be ready to explain how it worked, to investigate complaints, and to make improvements. In particular, all reports of the Academic Honesty Board should include a detailed list of plagiarized or falsified passages with documentation demonstrating the plagiarism or fraud, if necessary with an explanation of how the dishonesty was significant. The overall goal of improving universities, research, and academic honesty would be difficult to attack explicitly.

Although conservatives cannot realistically hope for universities with proportions of conservative and liberal professors approximating those of the whole population, the proposals outlined here could at least offer the prospect of less politicized universities. At present academic hiring takes place behind closed doors through an unsystematic and inequitable process that is seldom scrutinized by anyone. Ratings of dissertations by the Dissertation Review Board should make clear whenever hirings were flagrantly biased. For example, the ratings might well show that in some departments feminists were being hired in preference to less ideological women with much higher-rated dissertations, or that postmodernists were being hired in preference to less ideological scholars with much higher-rated dissertations. In the absence of any overall rating of candidates by qualifications, hiring any female or minority candidate can be defended as enhancing "diversity," hiring any postmodernist or feminist can be defended as putting the department "on the cutting edge," and both sorts of hires are hard to attack on grounds that they compromise quality. Since as matters stand it is much easier to tell who is black, female, postmodernist, or feminist than to tell who is good at teaching or research, many universities have been winning praise for promoting easily measured "diversity" and fashionability rather than unmeasured quality.

The Academic Honesty Board would be particularly likely to find plagiarism or fraud in the work of PhDs and professors who care less about scholarship than about ideology or deny the existence of objective truth. One notorious case of dishonesty was that of Ward Churchill, a tenured professor of ethnic studies at the University of Colorado who argued that the victims of the 2001 attack on the World Trade Center deserved to die because they were complicit in American foreign policy. Academic freedom protected his right to his views that American foreign policy was immoral and that collective guilt could justify mass murder; but he was still fired, despite his tenure, after a university committee found him guilty of plagiarism and falsifying data in his research. Some liberals have charged that his research received special scrutiny because of his political views.[5] It almost surely did. Yet as long as Churchill really was guilty of academic dishonesty, as even his defenders implicitly admitted, the injustice is not that he was investigated and dismissed; it is that others who are also guilty of academic dishonesty but have not expressed such unpopular opinions have not been investigated and dismissed. A National Academic Honesty Board would help correct that injustice, especially because in the absence of public outrage universities have no incentive to stir up scandals and controversies by investigating the honesty of their own PhDs and professors. Though not all academic dishonesty is equally unpopular, it is never harmless. Even if the dishonest research does no physical harm, as it certainly can do in medicine, it can spread errors and give the dishonest researcher an unfair advantage over honest researchers in competing for jobs, promotions, and grants. Dishonest research can also waste large amounts of federal, foundation, and university money.[6]

If the United States government can inspect and grade food and drugs and examine the competence of elementary and secondary teachers and students, why should it not examine and evaluate doctoral dissertations and academic publications? The Obama administration once proposed federal rankings of American colleges and universities on such dubious criteria as graduation rates and graduate earnings.[7] Some of the most perceptive critics of American universities have despaired of imposing any form of accountability on them because of institutional resistance and disputes over methods.[8] The failure of most students to learn much is admittedly the result of a combination of factors that are hard to distinguish from one another: bad college admissions, a bad curriculum, bad requirements for majors, poor study habits, easy grading, and the poor performance of many teaching assistants and professors in many different courses. Although most people would agree that the quality of the teaching assistants and professors is the most important factor, the majority, or at least those who see that student teaching evaluations measure popularity rather than effectiveness, have despaired of judging university teachers. Evaluating the quality of doctoral dissertations and the honesty of academic publications may not be the ideal method of judging professors, but it probably is the best method that is feasible. Since we require graduate students to spend several years of hard work writing dissertations, we should care how good their dissertations are, and we should hire those who have written the best dissertations in preference to those who have written worse ones.

Other Legislation

Even if no other law would improve American higher education as much as establishing federal boards to evaluate dissertations and the honesty of academic work, some other legislation could certainly help. One improvement would be a percentage cap on administrative costs as a condition for a university's keeping its tax-exempt status as a nonprofit institution. The high administrative costs of colleges and universities have been a largely overlooked scandal for years. In 2007 average administrative costs were about 19 percent for all institutions, 17.3 percent for public institutions, and 21.7 percent for private institutions. At Wake Forest University, a particularly shocking case, administration took up 53.7 percent of the budget. (In 2015 Wake Forest's president earned $4 million, more than any other college president in the country.)[9] By contrast, at the University of Michigan administrative costs were only 8.4 percent of the budget. Yet the *U.S. News* rankings for 2007, although skewed in favor of private universities like Wake Forest and against public universities like Michigan, ranked Wake Forest fortieth among national universities in quality and Michigan twenty-fourth. Princeton, ranked first in quality in 2007 by *U.S. News*, spent 29.6 percent of its budget on administrative costs, while Harvard, ranked second in 2007, spent 39.9 percent and Yale, ranked third, spent 32.5 percent. Of the three universities tied for fourth place in quality in 2007, Cal Tech spent only 5.0 percent of its budget on administrative costs, MIT 27.6 percent, and Stanford 17.5 percent. Therefore, the benefits, not to mention the necessity, of the higher percentages spent on administration are very far from clear. The Goldwater Institute, which compiled this information, held up Michigan as an example of what could be done to reduce administrative costs.[10]

Derek Bok, president of Harvard from 1971 to 1999, describes his own attempt after "several years in office" to reduce increases in administrative expenses there:

> I decided simply to inform our five vice presidents that, hereafter, their budgets could rise only by a percentage slightly higher than the anticipated rate of inflation but below the average rate of increase in

the budgets of the several faculties. If a vice president felt that there were compelling reasons for increasing expenses more rapidly than the target figure, he or she would have to persuade the other vice presidents to lower their costs to absorb the increase. If no agreement could be reached, the problem would come to me for resolution. Over the next decade, the system worked as planned. The central administration budget absorbed a gradually diminishing share of total university expenses. Thanks to an exceptional group of vice presidents, I was almost never called upon to resolve a budgetary impasse.

Bok considers his solution "too arbitrary to be a model for other institutions," because it may have prevented desirable expenditures and missed opportunities to reduce costs further.[11] Yet the ease with which Harvard restrained the growth of its administrative costs strongly indicates that they could actually have been *cut* without doing any harm. Nor is it clear that such "arbitrary" measures would have worse consequences at other institutions than they did at Harvard.

One possible exception is administrative activities that make money. Harvard's high administrative spending includes unusually large expenses for fund-raising and management of an enormous investment portfolio, all of which, Bok says, "seems justified so long as the extra personnel enable the institution to raise more than enough additional dollars to cover the incremental costs."[12] Interestingly, however, even the Harvard development office appears to have managed to live comfortably with the modest increases Bok allowed. If actual reductions had been put into effect, especially if they were large ones, spending less on the development office might well have cost more money than it was worth. Yet if reductions were required in the total percentage of administrative costs, with administrators allowed to decide how those cuts should be allocated, presumably administrators in other areas would have chosen to cut the development office less or not at all, if it raised more money than it spent. After all, the alternative would be either to suffer a loss in total university income that would further reduce money for administration or to forfeit a gain in total university income that would mitigate or even eliminate the reductions in money available for administration.

To exempt fund-raising and portfolio management from a cap on administrative expenses, and lowering the cap in proportion, would almost certainly be a mistake. Administrators are already much too eager to think that the main purpose of a university is to raise money, that a large endowment is a university's most important achievement, that programs should be judged by their appeal to potential donors rather than by their educational value, and that any of the university's problems should be addressed not by substantive reforms but by better publicity and public relations. Administrators are already much too reluctant to tell their development officers that a fund-raising campaign is too costly for the revenue it generates, that a superficially attractive program or building that might appeal to donors has no academic value, or that money should be spent on education instead of being added to the endowment or kept in the endowment.

A sympathetic study of Harvard—which has much the largest endowment of any university in the world—admits that its administrators seem to regard "having a large and growing endowment" as "an end in itself," remarking, "The average distribution rate to the faculties between 1971 and 1996 was a super-prudent 4.6 percent, leaving plenty to plow back into the endowment."[13] Exempting the development office from a cap applied to the rest of the administration would both insulate the development office from deserved criticism and increase its influence over administrators. On the other hand, a law requiring universities to spend a specified percentage of their endowments every year, as some have proposed, would attract strong opposition from administrators without any likely benefits. If forced, most administrators would simply spend the money either on themselves or on more fund-raising to ensure that their endowments continued to rise.

However, any attempt to impose a percentage limit on spending for university administration must explicitly define what can be counted as administrative costs. While the University of Michigan reported spending only 8.4 percent of its budget on administration, it also spent a mere 16.8 percent on instruction, 16.3 percent on research, and an astonishing 58.6 percent on "other." One may legitimately wonder whether Michigan's "other" category, which in any case seems absurdly high, includes expenses that other universities would count under administration. Any percentage caps on administrative expenses would obviously tempt administrators to find ways to label their expenses as something other than administrative. For example, if universities hired outsiders to perform certain administrative functions for a fee, such outsourcing could well reduce costs and increase efficiency, but that fee should still be counted as an administrative expense. By the same token, limits on administrative salaries would be even easier to evade than a limit on total administrative costs, because lower salaries can be supplemented by bonuses, free or subsidized housing, retirement plans, and similar perquisites, which may be justifiable but should certainly count as administrative expenses. Moreover, fewer and better-paid administrators may be preferable to a horde of lower-paid administrators. The public interest, expressed by legislation, should not be in managing the details of university administration but in ensuring that nonprofit universities devote most of their resources to teaching and research rather than to administration.

In fact, having an overly large and meddlesome administration usually harms teaching and research, because administrators without legitimate functions think of useless programs to keep themselves busy, distracting their faculty and students from education. Administrators love to require faculty to follow bureaucratic rules, fill out paperwork, attend worthless seminars and training sessions, and participate in projects that look glamorous but have no educational value and often make education worse. Such projects include dormitories with racial themes, study abroad programs that replicate an American campus in foreign countries, most community service programs, most online courses, most educational technology, and many conferences and ceremonies. As a general rule, if a program has a legitimate educational purpose, some professors will ask the administration for it, but if the initiative comes from the administration, the program has no legitimate educational purpose. The same is true of most new campus buildings: if the administration wants a new building but the faculty does not, the building is probably unnecessary and may well be worse than an existing building or a renovated building.

The exact limit that should be placed on administrative costs is a subject for legitimate debate. Yet if Cal Tech can make do with 5 percent and Stanford with 17.5 percent, nothing over 20 percent of the total university budget should be necessary. This is actually a little above the national average, though slightly below the average for private institutions. Any limit could of course be phased in gradually for extreme cases like Wake Forest and Harvard, perhaps in equal annual reductions over no more than five years. Any new colleges and universities should be exempt from this law for their first ten years, because they would need to have an administration before they could set up a campus, hire faculty, and admit students. For-profit institutions would naturally not be affected, having no tax exemptions to lose. Given the widespread concern over student debt and rising costs in higher education, passing such a law is probably politically feasible as a cost-cutting measure. Faculty would be unlikely to oppose it, since it would allocate more resources to teaching and research. The main opposition would come from university administrators, but this would rightly be discounted as self-serving.

Other laws are needed to protect lower-income students from incurring student debts they cannot repay. Though the Obama administration's proposal to rate institutions by the earnings of their graduates was misguided for most colleges and universities, at least it recognized that some institutions that claim to be preparing their students for jobs are failing to do so effectively. While no liberal arts graduates expect to get jobs as liberal artists, and many college graduates voluntarily take low-paying public service jobs or go on to graduate school before entering the job market, graduates of programs to train secretaries or physical therapists do expect to become secretaries or physical therapists. Students almost always enter this sort of program in order to get a job when they graduate, often taking out government-backed loans that they hope to repay from their salaries. Although students in such schools who do poor work, get poor grades, and are not hired have no one to blame but themselves, these schools have failed if most of their graduates with high grades fail to get the jobs they were trained for. A special accreditation board for such vocational programs should be able to determine fairly easily which schools are providing their best students with valuable credentials and which are not. A federal law should set up such an accreditation board for vocational programs and prohibit government grants and government-backed loans for programs that fail to receive the board's accreditation. The law should also promptly end eligibility for federal grants and loans for students who receive grades that are too low to qualify them for jobs.

Most of these vocational programs would probably be forced to shut down when their loss of accreditation makes them ineligible for government grants and loans and ruins their reputations. Unions at some community colleges and lobbyists for some for-profit schools are likely to resist such legislation, but Congress should be able to pass it despite their objections. What would be grossly unfair and unrealistic is to rate such institutions on the basis of their graduation rates, as the Obama administration suggested. None of them is well positioned to be selective in their admissions, and many community colleges are required by law to admit any high school graduate, no matter how poorly prepared or weakly motivated. The only way such institutions can train their students properly and provide them with meaningful credentials is to give low grades to students who are unwilling or unable to learn the material, most of whom should either drop out or graduate with grades that show how poorly prepared they are. Encouraging them to stay by giving them inflated grades deceives potential employers, discredits the institution, and devalues the credentials of properly prepared students. While this problem affects a minority of American institutions of higher education, it harms a significant group of relatively poor and poorly educated students who find themselves with high student debts but nearly worthless credentials. Since most such students lack the expertise to judge the value of the education they are borrowing to finance, government intervention is needed to keep them from making a costly mistake that will also waste government money.

Another law that would benefit such students but might be more difficult politically is a prohibition of government-subsidized loans for those without the basic preparation for a higher education. Bok sums up the view of several experts that "fewer than half of all high school graduates are capable of succeeding at a four-year college," and that in 2000 this number was "slightly *lower*" (italics his) than the number of "high school graduates who actually enrolled that year as freshmen in four-year colleges."[14] Matters are even worse at two-year colleges. Remedial courses have a poor record of overall success. Although borderline cases naturally exist, high school transcripts and test scores can clearly identify many students as unprepared for college, and the overwhelming majority of these students do indeed fail to graduate, often after taking out student loans that have done them no good and that they cannot afford to repay. They are wasting their time and money.[15] Yet most have never been told that they have very little chance of graduating, and many have actually been encouraged to go to college (by President Obama, among others). Unfortunately, attempts to deny loans to even the most hopeless cases can be characterized as denying them opportunities, and would endanger the existence of many two-year and for-profit colleges that have their own employees and defenders. As a result, legislation that would significantly restrict loans to unqualified students might be harder to pass than legislation that stigmatizes vocational programs for their failure rather than stigmatizing failing students. Yet no such political obstacles would block legislation establishing a National Dissertation Review Board and a National Academic Honesty Board or limiting spending on college and university administrations.

Chapter 7

A PROPOSAL FOR A UNIVERSITY

A New University

The decline and confusion that afflict our universities today are the results not of a reasoned debate but of a herd instinct, a sense of inevitability, and intellectual intimidation. These trends mostly began with fashions at a handful of leading universities—especially Harvard, Princeton, Yale, Stanford, and Berkeley—and have spread to a great extent through their influence. These five universities are in a class by themselves. The four that are private have by far the largest endowments of any universities in the country, ranging in 2016 from Princeton's $22 billion to Harvard's $35 billion.[1] (They also have the highest endowments per student.)[2] Since a university's attractiveness to donors reflects its prestige, endowment size is more an effect of that prestige than a cause. These universities are known not just for their academic quality—in which they have usually declined less than others because they have so much money that they can afford to spend some of it on academics— but also for their leading roles in American higher education. Reversing the deterioration of academic quality and academic freedom that these universities have started will require leadership by institutions with a position of influence comparable to theirs. Yet none of these five shows any real signs of intellectual recovery; instead they show every sign of sinking still deeper into leftist intolerance and mediocrity. No existing university is willing and able to challenge them. Might it be possible to found a new leading university that could and would challenge them and have comparable influence?

A moment's reflection should confirm how strange it is that no leading university has been founded in the United States since Stanford in 1891.[3] Since then American education has expanded exponentially. Senator Leland Stanford, before founding his university, had a fortune that (adjusted for inflation) would not even put him among *Forbes*'s 400 richest Americans today, when the country has more and richer donors than ever before. In 2015 donors gave a record $40.3 billion to higher education, more than the total endowment of Harvard ($35 billion) and almost double the endowments of Stanford or Princeton ($22 billion each).[4] Many donors are troubled by most universities' hostility to free speech, capitalism, religion, and traditional education, but, with no good university of a different sort to support, they either donate to existing universities or to other causes or keep their money. Sometimes they try to earmark their donations in ways that they hope will improve education in some respect, though usually they make only the most marginal difference or no difference at all. Some donors give money to small colleges, but even the best of these have next to no influence on the rest of American higher education, and their graduates find themselves with more limited opportunities than graduates of Harvard, Princeton, Yale, Stanford, and other elite institutions. When I taught at Hillsdale, its president talked about turning it into "the conservative Amherst." Yet Amherst is far from being at the forefront of American education or of American educated opinion. What is needed is not another and better Amherst, but another and better Harvard or Princeton.

A new leading university with a full range of academic programs would not need to be larger than Princeton, which has around 1,000 professors, 5,000 undergraduates, and 2,500 graduate students. (Princeton's administrative staff of roughly 1,000 is much larger than it needs to be.) Above that approximate minimum, which is larger than any small liberal arts college, size ceases to be an advantage: Princeton is a far more important, prestigious, and influential university than Arizona State University, which has ten times as many students and faculty. An initial donation of perhaps $1 billion, a sum within the means of many wealthy Americans, should attract enough additional donations to make a new university a reality. Paying for such a university would become much easier if it were to be founded (as Stanford was) as part of a new university town that would be an inviting place for its students and faculty to work and live. American university towns are now so attractive to so many potential residents that a new university town would be highly profitable for its developers, who should help fund the university.

Naturally donors would want to know to what sort of university they were giving their money. An initial donation of several million dollars would be enough to finance a planning group for a new university, with office space, a small staff, a travel budget, and fees for outside consultants and fund-raisers. The planning group could include professors from the National Association of Scholars as well as other experts on higher education who favored the project. Most of these would not always need to meet in one place, but could be brought in for regular meetings and otherwise consulted by telephone or teleconference. This group could be given a deadline of one or two years to prepare and publish a plan for the new university, with a deadline of five years to found the university if sufficient funds were pledged for it. Besides estimates of the basic costs of each stage of the university's development and a proposed location, the plan should include an administrative structure, a tentative undergraduate curriculum, and procedures for hiring deans and faculty. What follows, which is meant to stimulate rather than to limit discussion, outlines some of my own ideas about what such plans might be and what such a university might become. At the least, these ideas may serve to show what our universities might be that they now are not.

The new university's guiding aims should be to offer students the best possible education, to hire the best available professors, and to do the best possible research. Though these aims may seem obvious, right now they appear not to be those of any of the major universities in the country, all of which are worried about being labeled "elitist" and give priority to "diversity" and "inclusiveness" rather than "meritocracy." None is trying to become the best university in the country (though Harvard and Princeton each assume that they already are the best, with some justification in view of the competition). The new university should make every effort to become the very best according to traditional criteria. While the university should respect non-Western cultures, it should also recognize that America is a part of Western civilization, that Western civilization has much more influence in the world today than any other culture, and that America is more influential than any other country. Although the university should recognize that both America and Western civilization have their defects, it should openly prefer democracy, free speech, and freedom of religion, criteria by which America and the West are at present far ahead of China, Russia, and most African and predominantly Muslim countries. The university should also recognize Christianity and Judaism as prominent and valuable features of Western civilization.

The new university should be traditional in character but not specifically "conservative" in politics. It should generally avoid committing itself as an institution to any specific positions on current affairs, though its members, including its president and deans, should feel free to express their own political opinions, which ought to differ from each other. The only public positions the university should take on specific issues would be on matters that affect the free operation of universities, such as affirmative action, procedures for judging cases of sexual harassment, or restrictions on free speech and free association. The only ideologies the university should deliberately discourage are postmodernism, deconstructionism, and other relativistic doctrines that insist that nothing is objectively true and everything is an instrument of power, because such ideas rule out an honest search for the truth. The university should seek faculty and students who are interested in academics as such, not just as a vehicle for ideological expression and activism.

Although the university should welcome students and faculty of any religion or none, it would do well to dedicate itself formally to traditional Christianity and Judaism, as most private universities have done in the past. Recent years have shown that an absence of religion in public life can quickly turn into hostility to religion and that the main organized groups defending the right to hold moral views outside the leftist consensus are religious. Unfortunately, in America today much of public opinion and a growing body of law have come to assume that (apart from bigotry) religion is the only reason to hold beliefs such as that men are significantly different from women, abortion is wrong, or homosexuality is unnatural. The new university should nonetheless defend the rights of all students and citizens to express unfashionable views, whether or not they are based on religion. The university would need a strong legal department to contest the many government regulations that are incompatible with free speech and academic quality.

While the university should have a statement of principles, it should not have a "mission statement," which in academics has truly become the last refuge of the scoundrel. Mission statements imply that universities should change the world, but the main purpose of a university should be to provide its students with an excellent education. Of course members of universities may develop ideas for doing such things as relieving hunger or reducing environmental pollution, but actually doing those things is no more the function of a university than opening restaurants is the function of a farm or building highways is the function of an automobile manufacturer. Most university mission statements either consist of meaningless bromides or needlessly interfere with the university's activities and ambitions; surprisingly often, they manage to be both meaningless and intrusive, because nobody is sure how they might be interpreted. A university's policies should be designed to provide the best conditions for education, not to further the policies or interests of any political, racial, sexual, or environmental group. The main identity that the university should encourage among its students and faculty is that of a thoughtful and educated person, not of an ideologue or a member of a race, class, sex, or other group.

Since almost all major universities now discriminate systematically against moderates, conservatives, religious believers, and people interested in traditional education, a new university that put academic freedom and quality first should be able to attract some outstanding professors and students from leading universities and lesser universities. It should also appeal to professors and students at more conservative institutions where academics are now undervalued. The new university's professors, if hired with care, would on average be more independent-minded and more accomplished than the professors at today's leading universities, and unlike those professors would represent a spectrum of views as wide as that of educated people outside academia. Concentrating excellent moderate and conservative professors at a university that encouraged and rewarded them could create a powerful intellectual community from professors now scattered among different institutions that intimidate and silence them. The national media, who now look for experts and opinion leaders at Harvard, Princeton, and Berkeley—but not at

Hillsdale, Baylor, or Ave Maria University—might well seek experts and opinion leaders at a new leading university, if only to gain a reputation for balanced coverage or to make news through lively debate.

America's leading universities owe their leading roles partly to some shared characteristics that a new university could emulate. For one thing, the locations of most leading universities fit what might be called the Oxbridge model: within reach of a politically and culturally important metropolis but not so near as to be overshadowed or absorbed by it. Just as Oxford and Cambridge are about an hour and a half away from London, so Princeton and Yale are within an hour and a half of New York, while Harvard, Stanford, and Berkeley are somewhat closer to the centers of the smaller metropolitan areas of Boston and San Francisco. All these universities dominate university towns of their own, which have their own personalities and range in population from Princeton's 29,000 to Oxford's 160,000. All these towns have attractive neighborhoods and combine many of the benefits of small towns with most of the amenities of big cities, together with the advantages offered by major universities. As a result, Oxford, Princeton, Stanford, and Berkeley have more distinct and cohesive academic communities than universities located within major cities like the University of London, the University of Chicago, Columbia, or UCLA. On the other hand, universities that are too far from major cities, and those near major cities of less political and cultural importance, are at a disadvantage in attracting national attention and in attracting the best students and faculty.

The best place for a new university would probably be the suburbs or exurbs of Washington, D.C., which now has no leading university.[5] Except for New York (whose metropolitan area already includes two leading universities, Princeton and Yale), Washington is the most important city in America's public life. It has unique connections to the news media, Congress, and government agencies that could give a new university influence and visibility in public affairs (besides opportunities for internships). Washington also has major resources to support a university, like the Smithsonian Institution, the National Gallery, the National Archives, and especially the Library of Congress. With access to the Library of Congress as well as to the large and growing number of books and periodicals available online, a new university could forgo the expense of assembling a great research library and could manage with a merely good library, which should be relatively affordable now that used books have become cheaper. (The university might be able to acquire a good core collection by buying the library of one of the better liberal arts colleges that are occasionally forced to close.) The Washington exurbs are also a promising location for a new college town, which could attract educated people not directly connected with the university. Within fifty miles—the distance from New York to Princeton—Washington still has suitable sites for such a town. Since the 1960s the successful planned towns of Reston in Virginia and Columbia in Maryland have both been developed within twenty-five miles of Washington, closer than Stanford is to San Francisco. No comparable locations are available near New York City.

The planning group should outline the university's curriculum. Except for a language requirement restricted to languages with important literatures, the university should avoid "distribution requirements," which force students to choose from lists of specialized courses in various fields. (For example, students at Harvard can now satisfy their general requirement in "Aesthetic and Interpretive Understanding" with such courses as "American Dreams from *Scarface* to *Easy Rider*.") In many universities these requirements now make a coherent education almost impossible by forcing students to take overly specialized and doctrinaire courses. If all students should know something about a subject, they should be required to take a general survey course on it. Survey courses required of all students should concentrate on material that will remain important throughout the students' lifetimes. These courses should give minimal attention to the most recent developments in the sciences, literature, art, and music, since most of today's scientific findings, novels, poems, artworks, and musicians will be of merely nostalgic interest by the time today's students reach middle age.[6] Students should take the survey courses as freshmen, since what they learn in them might well affect their choice of majors at the end of their freshman year.

The main outlines of a good program in general education should be obvious to anyone without a bias against Western civilization. Examples can be found in the program in Contemporary Civilization long required at Columbia and the Common Core required at the University of Chicago before it was diluted some time ago. The required courses should include great books that every educated person should have read, and the reading lists should be the same or very similar for all students to give them a common foundation of knowledge. Contrary to present practice at most universities, the new university should encourage survey courses on all significant subjects and discourage idiosyncratic courses on narrow and fashionable topics. The university also ought to adopt guidelines for its undergraduate majors, which should ban departmental distribution requirements, encourage tutorials and survey courses, and allow some courses to be prerequisites for others, but otherwise leave students wide discretion to plan their own courses of study.

Establishing the University

As soon as enough money had been raised to ensure that the university would become a reality, the planning group could convert itself, with appropriate changes, into a board of trustees. It should choose a university president, preferably a well-respected scholar with enthusiasm for what the university is trying to do, though an exception might be made for a well-educated public figure with the same enthusiasm and special talents as a fund-raiser and spokesman, roles that would also be important. The board should choose a dean of the faculty with strong academic credentials and intellectual vision, rendering the appointment of a provost unnecessary.[7] The administration should be kept as small as possible. To avoid giving the impression that the university was modeling itself on a profitable business corporation, titles like CEO or vice president should be avoided. The overall curriculum would help determine the number of professors in each department. The president, dean of the faculty, and trustees should give special care to hiring a dean of admissions and department chairmen, who should be not just outstanding scholars but also gifted talent scouts. All the deans should be professors in one of the university's departments, with ranks corresponding to their academic achievements. Administrators' salaries should never be more than half again as much as those of the best-paid regular professors. In order to discourage the growth of a special class of administrators, professors should frequently move in and out of university administration. All the university's plans should be subject to constant revision in the light of experience.

Henry Rosovsky, a former dean of the faculty of Harvard with whom I often disagree, makes one excellent suggestion for improving universities: "Increasing the authority and dignity of department chairmen."[8] The chairmen should have the primary responsibility for hiring faculty in their departments, not just at first but permanently. A major problem with academic hiring today is that no single person is responsible for any department as a whole, so professors choose their colleagues on the basis of their own self-interest, likes, and dislikes rather than the interests of their department, students, or university. (Unfortunately, even some highly distinguished scholars can be biased, careless, or petty in making hiring decisions.) Finding distinguished scholars who are willing to hire scholars at least as good as themselves is hard, but it needs to be done only once for each department if the department chairman controls hiring. Naturally the chairman should consult other department members who know something about the candidates and their fields, but the final appointment should not depend on a bare majority vote of professors without expert knowledge of the candidates' specialty. Each department chairman should decide, along with the trustees, on the departmental requirements for student majors and a long-term plan for hiring professors to teach the courses needed for the department's majors, other interested students, and the overall curriculum. This plan should of course be subject to revisions as the university and its departments developed.

The university should begin its hiring by requesting applications for every field and rank, soliciting additional applications, and hiring the very best applicants the first year while keeping other outstanding applications in reserve for the next year or two. Later positions advertised should be broadly defined (e.g., "classical philosophy" rather than "Plato"), usually leaving the professorial rank open, in order to attract the broadest possible pool of applicants. The department chairmen should actively recruit outstanding scholars who might not otherwise apply, including scholars from foreign countries with a good command of English and scholars not currently employed at colleges and universities. While attention should be given to speaking and teaching skills, the main grounds for hiring professors should be their records of research and publication, measured by the criteria of originality, importance, accuracy, rigor, and clarity described earlier.[9] A professor who has written original, important, accurate, rigorous, and lucid books and articles is almost certain to be a good teacher of good students (though not necessarily of bad students, who should not go to a leading university). Such a professor will also probably have things to say that will be heard outside the university.

If properly applied, these criteria should exclude narrow specialists, rigid ideologues, and convinced postmodernists. The minimum requirement for hiring an assistant professor should be one important research project, either published or accepted for publication as a book or series of articles. The minimum requirement for a tenured associate professor should be two such projects, which should also be the requirement for granting tenure (twice the tenure requirement at most universities, which typically require just one book or one series of articles). The minimum requirement for a full professor should be three such projects (again, one more than at most universities). Letters of recommendation have become such debased currency that they should be given little weight, but one should probably be requested, since a recommender can include some relevant things that an applicant cannot easily say about himself.[10] Applicants should be promised that their names will not be divulged if they are not hired, since otherwise they might well be reluctant to apply for fear of identifying themselves as conservatives or moderates. Favoritism of any sort should be avoided as much as possible.

Professorial salaries at the new university should be appreciably higher on average than the salaries paid at established leading universities. These salaries should allow professors hired away from leading universities to be compensated for uprooting themselves and their families and moving to a new institution with a still-developing reputation; yet other equally deserving professors should be paid no less. Generous moving allowances and provisions for housing should be included in all job offers. The salary scale should be made public, with clearly defined ranks and the same salary for every professor at each rank, ranging for example from Assistant Professor I to Full Professor XII. Each professor's rank should be based on his academic and intellectual accomplishments over his whole career to date, and the professor should rise in rank as he accomplishes more. Most of his accomplishments would be academic publications, but other publications and activities such as service as department chairman should also be recognized. This sort of salary scale, now used in the University of California system, is far superior to the annual reviews and percentage raises that determine academic salaries at most universities, which tend to perpetuate accidental inequities.[11]

Significant deficiencies in teaching, particularly giving inflated grades, should be penalized as suggested earlier.[12] Department chairmen should monitor teaching, but any system of student teaching evaluations should be run only by students, not by the university. If a husband and wife are both outstanding scholars, both should be hired; if one is outstanding and the other is less qualified, the other should be given the unsalaried rank of research associate with academic privileges such as access to library resources. (Similar accommodations need not be made for unmarried partners, since professors should not expect the university to commit itself to hire someone they will not commit themselves to marry, though such partners could still be hired on their merits.) Adjunct professors should be few (and mostly not academics, like retired politicians, government officials, and military officers) and paid regular professorial salaries adjusted for their teaching loads and qualifications (that is, more than ten times what most adjuncts receive now). The president and dean of the faculty should study each department chairman's hiring recommendations carefully and reject any candidates who are less than outstanding. When necessary, the president and dean should be ready to replace department chairmen, who would of course remain tenured professors.

Students should be admitted on the basis of primarily academic criteria. Although test scores, high school grades, and essays can be useful indicators, the most reliable means of identifying applicants with strong intellectual interests is usually to have them interviewed by members of the admissions staff, who could also help recruit applicants at the crucial early stage when the university is still establishing its reputation. This would require hiring an unusually competent admissions staff, most of whom should be graduate students or recent PhDs without regular academic positions. The admissions staff should give little if any weight to some criteria favored by most admissions officers elsewhere, such as ethnicity, "volunteer" work (especially mandatory "volunteer" work), and extracurricular activities unrelated to intellectual concerns. The admissions staff should visit as many high schools as possible and take special care to interview homeschooled students, who are often excellent and strongly committed to academics. Staff members should be allowed to offer particularly well-qualified applicants full scholarships regardless of need and should offer travel, living, and book allowances to those from the lowest-income families. Foreign students with a good knowledge of English should be encouraged to apply and should be interviewed whenever possible.

While admitting all applicants with the finest overall academic qualifications, the university should also admit some with extraordinary abilities in some academic fields and less in others—that is, students who are not necessarily "well-rounded." Thus the inspired but innumerate poet and the brilliant but inarticulate physicist should usually be admitted, along with the dyslexic or autistic Renaissance man. The university should also seek students who are likely to choose a wide variety of different majors, as determined by the interests they mention when they apply. Since a university is among other things a social community, some attention should be given to students' personalities, at least by holding antisocial applicants to slightly higher intellectual standards than others. Again for social reasons, an effort should be made to keep the student body from being lopsidedly male or female.[13] Such adjustments should never lead to rejecting any outstanding students or to admitting any undistinguished students. The goal should be to select those most eager and best prepared to receive an excellent education. Easily offended students or students who insist on saving the world before learning about it should be encouraged to go elsewhere.

Undergraduates should be required, and graduate students should be encouraged, to live on campus. If the university were part of an intelligently planned university town, many of the faculty and administrators would live near the students, served by a city government, schools, police, churches, restaurants, shops, and other businesses suited to the university's particular needs. In the town as on the campus, monumentality should be avoided in favor of livability. The town could be designed as a compromise between the current urban and suburban models of living, offering apartments, row houses, and detached houses to meet the preferences of different residents and accommodating pedestrians, motorists, and cyclists without pitting them against each other. Private businesses and residences should be near and could even be scattered among the university buildings, as is the case at Oxford, Cambridge,

Harvard, Yale, and some other great universities. Appropriate models for a university town can be found in Princeton, Palo Alto, Oxford, and both Cambridges.

Since the university would soon grow too large to be a place where everyone knew everyone else, it would need smaller divisions, like Oxford and Cambridge colleges, Harvard houses, Yale colleges, Princeton eating clubs, or fraternities and sororities at other universities. Unfortunately, most such units in American universities have failed to develop the sense of community of Oxbridge colleges, chiefly because university administrators have tried to prevent students from forming groups by common interests, race, class, drinking habits, or anything else.[14] Many of the administrators' efforts are understandable, because the units with the strongest sense of community are usually fraternities and sororities and ethnic theme houses, all of which tend to be cliquish and anti-intellectual. The main problem is that, unlike the Oxbridge colleges, none of these units at American universities has any real function in the process of education, which in America is chiefly run by academic departments.

The best solution would be to have departmental colleges, with residences, dining halls, classrooms, and faculty offices organized around groups of related departments.[15] A university of about 5,000 undergraduates might have ten or so such colleges, with an average of about 100 professors, 375 upperclassmen, and 250 graduate students each. Some graduate students and junior faculty could serve as tutors and live in the departmental colleges with the undergraduates. Such colleges would have their own bedrooms, classrooms, dining halls, athletic facilities, faculty offices, student and faculty common rooms, and specialized libraries. Freshmen who had yet to declare their majors and were taking required survey courses could live in a large freshman college with a separate dining hall and athletic facilities. Other university facilities could be grouped around the departmental colleges, including a central library, student center, faculty club, and auditoriums for larger classes, assemblies, films, and special events.

The student center and faculty club should be attractively laid out, including private dining rooms, lounges, exercise machines, handball and tennis courts, and a swimming pool—but expensive facilities used by only a few obsessive enthusiasts should be avoided. The food at the student dining halls and faculty club should be varied, healthy, and good. Professors should be offered free parking and a free lunch in the faculty club every weekday to encourage them to come to campus for more than just their classes and office hours. The president should have a house on campus, and the master of each college should have a residence in the college. Professors should be encouraged to live near to the campus with the incentives of housing subsidies and favorable leases on university-owned houses.

Since the intellectual life of the university would be built around the departmental colleges, defining them is important. They should include no vocational departments—for example, a Department of Economics but not a Department of Business Administration. They should exclude departments of women's studies or ethnic studies, which would become ideological and ethnic ghettoes, like ethnic theme houses in other American universities.[16] However, area studies departments such as classics and Near Eastern studies have an obvious reason for their existence, because classical and Near Eastern languages are particularly hard to learn, and without learning them classical and Near Eastern history and literature cannot be studied rigorously. Groups of science departments would have their own colleges, with laboratories along with other academic and residential facilities. The college with the art, drama, and music departments should include studios and theaters. The colleges could best be arranged around one or more quadrangles, a form that evolved from the monastic cloister and is found at Oxford and Cambridge and many American universities. The quadrangle is a particularly good arrangement for combinations of academic and residential buildings, including a garden or lawn and trees in the middle.

All students should have private rooms, no matter how small, to keep roommates from disturbing each other's studying or sleep. Insulation should be thick, but loud music or other noise should still be prohibited. Bathrooms could be shared, but not by both sexes. Hallways and entryways should be segregated by sex. The university should resist legislative and other attempts to impose the new and bizarre view that the sexes are not significantly different, and it should not admit transsexual students who demand special treatment. Reasonable dietary restrictions should be accommodated in the dining halls. Regular cleaning should be included in room charges, since students are seldom good housekeepers but ought not to live in squalor. The common rooms in the departmental colleges should be comfortable, without televisions or computers but with fireplaces with gas fires in the winter. Everything should be arranged as far as possible to promote intellectual activity and conversation among students and faculty.

The curriculum should encourage intellectual life on campus by giving all students an important store of knowledge in common. Campus activities that would contribute to education should also be encouraged or provided by the administration. Showings of classic films, concerts of classical music, special performances of plays, and lectures by prominent politicians and authors should all be tried—and should become regular features if they found significant audiences among the students and faculty. If not, the administration should resist the temptation to show action films and host rock concerts and talks by television personalities, not because these things are bad but because they make no contribution to an excellent education. The administration should encourage students to organize their own publications, websites, and clubs, which, contrary to the practice of many universities, should be allowed to exclude any students who oppose the group's purposes. If students wanted to organize a student government and could muster a majority of the student body to ratify a constitution for such a government, the administration should recognize it and cooperate with it; but any student dues should be voluntary, to avoid forced contributions to activities that the student might not want and might disapprove of.

Every student should be required before enrolling to subscribe to an honor code, which should include pledges never to engage in cheating or fraud and never to obstruct the free speech or free movement of anyone else. Peaceful picketing or assemblies should be protected, though not if they disrupted classes. The administration should draw up a process for investigating and punishing infractions of the honor code, and serious violations should be enforced by suspension or expulsion. Suspension or expulsion would, however, be too harsh a penalty for conduct that was merely irresponsible or inconsiderate. Deciding exactly what to do about underage drinking, misdemeanor drug use, and sexual activity is admittedly difficult for universities today. Many intellectuals have not been known for their restraint in drinking and sex, and future generations will be astonished that our laws consider most college-age students responsible enough to vote but too irresponsible to drink a glass of beer. The university should avoid currently fashionable sanctimoniousness about smoking, especially of relatively harmless electronic cigarettes, since smoking tobacco, unlike smoking marijuana, prevents nobody from studying. The university should prohibit cohabitation in campus rooms, if only as a distraction from studying. (Narrow beds should help discourage overnight stays.) The university, like American society as a whole, should recognize that some activities ought to be discouraged but not forbidden, rather than turning every form of behavior into either a crime or a civil right.

Rape, assault, murder, driving while intoxicated or drugged, and major thefts are crimes, not mere disciplinary infractions, and should be investigated and punished not by the university but by the police and the courts. The campus police force should always have on duty at least one female officer with proper training in rape and assault cases, to whom victims of rape should be referred. This officer should advise victims on whether what has happened meets the legal definition of rape or assault and, if so, what should be done to collect evidence and to report the crime to the regular police. The university should offer appropriate help in investigations but should avoid prejudging cases, since a false charge of rape or assault also has severe consequences. If misguided government regulations force the university to try rape or assault cases, this should be done by specially hired lawyers and retired judges in a process as much like a regular court as possible.

Students convicted of rape, like those convicted of any other serious crime, should be expelled. In the absence of a charge of rape reported to the police, however, the university should as a rule avoid taking sides in sexual disputes among its students. It should also reject the idea that female students need or deserve more protection than other young women or are less likely to make false accusations. Students should be treated as much as possible as responsible adults, and responsible adults do not enter a bed with someone who is under the influence of alcohol or drugs or if they are themselves under such influence. If the university does its job well, most students should have little time for alcohol or drugs, and those who let drugs or alcohol affect their studies should soon be suspended or dismissed for academic reasons. The university should allow students to take a semester or a year off if they request it, and offer appropriate help to students who seek it. However, the university should avoid assuming the role of a rehabilitation facility.

The university should permanently rule out building or acquiring a campus abroad, which would be an expensive distraction from its academic community and could create serious problems for academic freedom if located in a country that restricts political or religious speech or activities. If students are going to sit in a classroom with their classmates, they can best do so on the university's campus in America.[17] If students want to do extensive charitable or political work at home or abroad, they should be encouraged to do it on a year off rather than trying to study at the same time. On the other hand, the administration should encourage professors to organize study tours abroad for students, their parents, other professors, and other friends of the university during vacations, reserving rooms in hotels of different classes and prices and chartering planes, ships, and buses to see important monuments, sites, and museums. As a rule the university should offer no online courses, which for most students are much inferior to good traditional courses. Exceptions might be made for courses in computer science for self-disciplined and computer-obsessed students, though such students might well be happier not attending a university at all.

The president and the dean of the faculty should try to become acquainted with as many of the professors in the university as possible. University and departmental parties can be helpful for this, now that private dinner parties have grown rare in American social life. The president and dean should host frequent dinners for twenty to thirty professors at the president's house or a private dining room in the faculty club, with food, drink, and waiters provided by the university. Since such dinners would be a part of academic life, as at Oxford and Cambridge, spouses should not be invited, and couples who are both professors should usually be invited to different dinners. All professors should be invited at least once to such dinners, which could also be held for groups of professors with common interests. Reasonable accommodations could be made for special dietary requirements by bringing in different meals for some diners. Antisocial professors could of course decline their invitations. Professors should be encouraged to meet for lunch and dinner at the faculty club and to host lunches and dinners there for their colleagues and students at university expense. A faculty

senate should be unnecessary, because meetings of the whole faculty
would be of manageable size and attract all the professors interested in
attending. Faculty committees, which are seldom representative of the
faculty and provide few benefits and many distractions, should be kept
to a bare minimum.[18]

The university should firmly resist forces that try to limit free speech
in the name of "diversity," "inclusivity," "sensitivity," and "equality" for
various minority groups and for the majority group of women. Without
breaking existing laws, the new university should protest and oppose
laws and court rulings that violate freedom of speech or prohibit conduct that ought to be protected in a free society. The university should
encourage basic courtesy in speech and behavior but otherwise should
not sympathize with those who protest that they are offended by the
speech or behavior of others, especially if the protesters are themselves
discourteous and offensive.[19] The university should also defend all
research and scholarship that is honestly done, even if such research con-
firms or refutes theories that some people oppose or support for political
reasons. In fact, the university should try to sponsor objective and rigorous research on topics that other universities avoid as too controversial,
like climate engineering, the consequences of family breakdown, and the
philosophical inconsistencies of collective guilt. The university should
have a campus newspaper and website run by students and financed by
the administration that would discuss a wide range of issues and publish
the opinions not only of students but of professors and administrators
as well. The university should limit its athletic programs to intramural
teams and to providing students and professors with facilities for exercise and recreation.[20] At some time in the future the university might
decide to start a law school, a medical school, a university press, a radio
station, a scholarly journal, or a sponsored opinion poll.

The importance such a university could have in American public
life is hard to overestimate. Today American academics have a strong
public voice that is predominantly leftist, largely self-serving, and cow-
ardly or hostile in questions of free speech and intellectual diversity.
Although some conservative think tanks and other organizations offer
different points of view and sponsor certain kinds of research, none of
them has the intellectual or financial resources, academic credentials,
or prestige of any of the country's leading universities. As a result, those

universities, and many leftist public figures, can simply ignore moderate and conservative opinions as partisan, biased, and poorly informed. No foundation or small college is in a position to rival the leading universities in influence, and none is able to train well-qualified future professors, as only major universities can. Nothing else any donor can do today could have nearly the long-term social, cultural, or political impact of helping to finance a new leading university. From the moment of its foundation, such a university could begin to transform the country's cultural and intellectual life.

Possible Objections

One objection to founding such a university might be that too few truly outstanding scholars could be found for its faculty. While the number of outstanding scholars has unfortunately dwindled because universities and colleges now discourage many kinds of good scholarship and many fine scholars have left the academic profession, my experience on search committees convinces me that a number of fine scholars are either still on the job market or teaching at institutions that they would be willing or happy to leave. These scholars are seldom offered jobs at prestigious universities because their work is considered unfashionable and their excellence makes hiring committees uncomfortable. Yet many such scholars are eventually hired somewhere, though they must often disguise or mute their moderate or conservative opinions in order to be hired or retained. As a result the exact size of the pool of outstanding traditional scholars is hard to estimate, but a large percentage of them would surely apply if an excellent new institution spread the word that it was looking for them and promised them confidentiality if they were not hired. As of now, the number available should be more than enough to staff a new university with a faculty of 1,000 or so. To increase the number of candidates, the university should concentrate on hiring for quality rather than for narrowly defined fields, since good scholars can usually teach capably outside their main research specialties.[21]

Another objection to founding this sort of university might be that it would remove good traditional scholars from other colleges and universities, making large and prestigious colleges and universities even more leftist and smaller and more conservative colleges and universities even less intellectually distinguished. This objection would obviously not apply to the new university's hiring scholars who had no regular jobs as professors; but relatively few excellent scholars remain in the academic profession for long without regular jobs, and those who have been away from the profession for any length of time are seldom prepared to return. Any reluctance to hire professors away from other institutions would seriously harm the quality and reputation of the new university, besides being unjust to excellent professors who wanted to join it. Of course, professors could choose to stay where they were for any reason, including that they thought they were helping to make distinguished institutions less leftist or to make conservative institutions more distinguished. Yet at least at the conservative institutions, the attraction of higher salaries, better opportunities for research, more national attention, and a livelier intellectual community would probably induce most candidates to accept offers from the new university. More prestigious institutions would be better able to compete in providing high salaries, opportunities for research, national attention, and an intellectual community, but the new university could still probably hire away some professors who were tired of being marginalized by left-wing colleagues. Sad to say, many universities would be delighted to see their few conservative professors depart.

As for the relatively few conservative institutions, most of them emphasize basic teaching and have little to offer serious scholars, who are largely wasted in such places. One benefit of a new university might be to persuade some conservative institutions to try to retain their more scholarly professors by giving them higher salaries and lighter teaching loads, instead of assuming (often correctly) that they have few opportunities elsewhere. Some Catholic universities are in a different category, because they are trying to shed their unfashionable Catholic identity and would be glad to see some of their orthodox Catholic professors leave for a new university. In most such universities, the battle for a Catholic identity has already been effectively lost, and any chance of improvement is too remote to justify encouraging orthodox Catholic scholars to remain marginalized and unappreciated there. On the other hand, Catholic institutions whose Catholic identity still means something to them might well be encouraged to strengthen that identity and to treat their orthodox Catholic scholars better if those scholars could otherwise be hired away by a new university. Though the new university may well have a connection with Christianity and Judaism, it should avoid hiring on the basis of religion or religious orthodoxy rather than academic merit; by contrast, religious universities ought sometimes to put denomination and orthodoxy first if they take their affiliations seriously.

As for the possibility that the new university might hire away the last relatively conservative scholars from large and predominantly leftist private and public universities, the answer is much the same as for most Catholic universities: relatively conservative scholars are now so few and so marginalized in these institutions that they do scarcely any good, and most of them would be much more effective and happier at a new university where they could speak their minds freely. Being one of a handful of dissenting voices in the classroom, in hiring, or in setting the curriculum is frustrating and almost useless, and it often attracts charges of "racism," "sexism," "homophobia," and "lack of commitment to the university's values." As a result, conservative and moderate professors usually remain silent even when they disagree with the prevailing ideology; at most they register their disagreement quietly, realizing that it will be ignored. If such institutions are ever to change, the best hope is to show them that an outstanding university can be built around the values of intellectual excellence, objective truth, and academic freedom. If this were demonstrated, faculty and administrators at the other universities, whose real motive is opportunism or cowardice rather than loyalty to "diversity," "inclusivity," Marxism, feminism, or postmodernism, might even decide that objective truth and academic freedom were new academic fashions that needed to be included. A bidding war between Harvard or Princeton and the new university for a distinguished traditional scholar would be an entirely healthy sign for American education.

Another objection to this sort of new university might be that it would discredit itself among other academics and intellectuals because its student body and faculty would be overwhelmingly white and Asian and disproportionately rich and male. Such a result would offend against "diversity," which has been recognized as highly desirable by a bare majority of the Supreme Court, which in turn has been slavishly followed by an overwhelming majority of today's academics. After all, if the new university tried to admit students and hire faculty on the basis of merit alone, while nearly all other universities took race and sex into account, the other universities would seem to have great advantages in recruiting the best black, Hispanic, and female students and faculty. In fact, however, today's academic hiring usually favors only black, Hispanic, and female applicants who hold the sorts of views that the universities approve. Women, blacks, and Hispanics who do not regard themselves as oppressed, or who want to study subjects unrelated to the group identities that they are supposed to share, often find themselves considered betrayers of their race and sex and are not hired, at least not at the more prestigious institutions. I suspect that the new university would be able to recruit significant numbers of female, black, and Hispanic faculty and students of this sort.

In any case, a new university should resist the fashionable dogma that something is wrong with a society unless every activity and profession has the same proportion of each race and sex as the population as a whole. Discrimination against women and minorities is virtually unknown in American higher education today and is certainly negligible in comparison with the discrimination *in favor of* women and minorities and against whites, Asians, men, and conservatives (sometimes including female and minority conservatives). On average women in America are more successful than men throughout their educational careers, getting better grades and attending college and graduating in larger numbers. That women with children tend to be less professionally successful than men is not a problem that can be solved by giving them preferential treatment in hiring—if indeed a choice to spend time away from a job in order to raise children should be considered a problem at all. That on average black and Hispanic Americans do worse in primary and secondary schools than whites and Asian Americans is a well-known and disturbing fact, but its main causes have been convincingly shown to be poor and mediocre teaching in predominantly black and Hispanic schools and the disproportionate breakdown of black and Hispanic families. Discrimination in favor of black and Hispanic candidates in admissions and hiring in higher education distracts attention from these fundamental problems and contributes nothing to solving them.

Another possible objection to this sort of university is the anti-intellectual one that it would be too relentlessly academic, and particularly that some of its academically ambitious students would become demoralized when they received lower grades than other students did.

The Harvard admissions office used to say that it wanted to admit a "happy bottom quarter" of the class, consisting of students who would be content with below-average grades because they had other interests, primarily in sports. The same argument could be made with more cogency in favor of fielding teams of mediocre athletes who would play badly and happily lose games. Education is not a game, in which only one player or the members of only one team can win. Universities should aim to give all their students a first-class education, though naturally some students will do better than others. The strategy of admitting students with interests outside academics has succeeded far too well at most universities, where few students have any genuine interest in academics apart from their grades. A university that worries that its students might be too interested in education makes no more sense than a hospital that worries that its patients might become too healthy. Few if any of the aimless partygoers on university campuses today used to have serious academic interests but abandoned them after getting poor grades. Students with serious academic interests are likely to be happiest at a university where academic interests are shared and encouraged.

A more sophisticated version of this anti-intellectual argument is that a university like the one proposed here would give too much attention to traditional academics, and particularly to academic departments, rather than to an "interdisciplinary" approach. My own interdisciplinary credentials are not bad, as a professor trained in a classics department and teaching in a history department, who majored as an undergraduate in history and literature, has held two joint appointments in history and classics, and has published two books on history, two on literature, and six on both history and literature. I nonetheless agree with Martin Trow when he wrote,

> Very few academics, even those who have achieved high distinction in their own field, have intellectual qualities that make for first-rate interdisciplinary teachers. When courses and programs are created in the face of these difficulties, they are very often short-lived failures; a genuine integration of perspective and knowledge around a problem or issue is rarely achieved, and such courses often descend to a lowest common denominator of relatively uninformed discussion among teachers and students, none of whom has a solid mastery of the

topic or its problems. As one scholar with experience has observed, "Interdisciplinary programs are devices for bringing creative people together and arranging for them to be less creative," at least in the short term.[22]

If a university has bad academic departments, it is a bad university, and the fault lies with the university and its departments, not with the idea of departments per se. Disciplines are called disciplines because they have their own rules, and interdisciplinary work too often attempts to avoid all rules. Good interdisciplinary work simultaneously follows the rules of every discipline it spans, and it therefore counts as good work within each discipline without needing to hide behind another one. To be sure, disciplinary boundaries can be changed or transcended, but in the absence of any boundaries education becomes a formless and unmanageable mass. Christopher Jencks and David Riesman, after examining the faults of many existing academic departments, rightly concluded, "A large academic community needs some sort of formal subgroupings around which individuals can cluster. The departments fill this need; that is the source of their power. If they were abolished, something would have to be put in their place."[23] Students should take courses in several departments and should be allowed to have joint majors if these form a coherent course of study. Some professors should be able to hold joint appointments and to teach courses cross-listed in more than one department. Appropriate joint appointments should be encouraged, not least because only a professor who knows two disciplines well can properly supervise students who are studying both of them. Joint majors who live in colleges among students in one of their two majors will do no worse in their other major—certainly no worse than if they were to live among students with no academic interests whatever.

Many people will surely think that starting a new university would be more difficult and expensive than reforming an old one. In theory, no doubt, enlightened trustees could choose a determined and forceful new president for an already distinguished university. This president could then choose new deans and department chairmen, giving them authority to appoint outstanding new faculty without interference from the existing faculty. The president could introduce a new and rigorous curriculum and new and rigorous guidelines for departmental majors. The president could choose a new dean of admissions with orders to admit only applicants with the best academic qualifications. The president could even reorganize the university into colleges composed of academic departments. Yet I am not aware of any existing major university that has such enlightened trustees. If one did, the president whom they chose would probably face a faculty revolt over the new curriculum, which old professors would oppose, and the new program of hiring, which would cost professors their power to choose their colleagues and would create a divided faculty, with new professors who were better qualified and better paid than the old ones. The faculty, though it might accept the new colleges and might applaud a new admissions policy that ended favoritism for athletes and the children of alumni, would still defend favoritism for black, Hispanic, and female faculty and students.

Many alumni, including those who helped interview applicants, would object to an admissions policy that gave no preference to their own children or to athletes who could make the difference between winning and losing teams. The present students would protest that the new policies favored academics instead of athletics, "service," and "social justice." Both students and faculty would protest the abandonment of the goal of "diversity" and leftist politics in general in favor of "elitism" and "meritocracy," and would complain that the president was "taking their university away from them." While a newly founded university could choose administrators, professors, and students who supported its new policies, reforms in an existing university would be a constant source of discord. Even if the trustees and president kept their nerve and managed to maintain their policies, only after fifteen to twenty years of rancor would the majority of the faculty have been hired under the new system. An extremely tactful and determined president of an older university might well be able to accomplish some part of what a new university could do, but with far more trouble. On the other hand, the example and competition of a successful new university would make such reforms in older universities much easier in the future.

Some reasonable people may still fear that a new university might discredit the cause of academic excellence and objectivity by not being good enough to compete with the best existing universities and to serve as an example for them. The founders of the new university should take such fears seriously and do everything possible to make the university truly distinguished. If they failed to raise enough money or to attract enough interest, they should abandon the project rather than add another failed university to those we already have. Yet America is a big country, filled with prosperous, intelligent, and enterprising people, and much of the rest of the world admires its achievements and sends a great many students and even substantial donations to American universities. Can it really be that there are not enough donors with enough money anywhere who care enough to found a great university committed to putting academic quality and academic freedom first? Can it really be that fewer than a thousand excellent students graduate from secondary schools each year who would want to attend such a university? Can it really be that fewer than a thousand excellent scholars can be found who would want to join such a university? At the least, if there is a real possibility that these conditions could be met, would a few million dollars be too much to spend on a planning group to find out?

Chapter 8

INSPIRING A RENAISSANCE

Cultural Brilliance

I begin my undergraduate course on ancient Greek history by telling my students something like this:

> Long ago, when I was a graduate student in classics (that is, ancient Greek and Roman history and literature), I used to resent people who studied ancient Greece and looked down on people who studied ancient Rome or (like me) studied the medieval Greeks (that is, the Byzantine empire). Those specialists in ancient Greece took for granted that ancient Greece was magic, absolutely unique, and superior to every other culture that ever was. Today I still study the Byzantine empire, and I think it's a very interesting subject. If you like, I'll be happy to teach it to you next year, when I'll offer a course on it. All the same, I should admit to you right now that the people I used to resent were right: ancient Greece *was* magic, absolutely unique, and superior to every other culture that ever was.

Cultural brilliance was of course not just a characteristic of ancient Greece but recurred in many different times and places throughout history. Exactly why it occurred at some times and places but not at others remains a question that few people study, even fewer are prepared to answer, and nobody has answered completely.[1] I was looking for the causes of cultural brilliance years ago when as a postdoctoral fellow at Stanford I organized a faculty seminar on "Renaissances Before the Renaissance," seven cultural revivals that happened in Late Antiquity and the Middle Ages.[2] I now think one reason the seminar largely failed to find the causes of the revivals was that, in an effort to keep the contributions in focus, I concentrated on only the first two centuries of recovery after each "dark age" when culture had taken a major step backward. As a rule, however, such dark ages did too much cultural damage to let collective brilliance ignite at once. What happened at first was usually a revival of learning, not a revival of literature. If that revival of learning was strong and sustained, great literature developed later, in the two centuries or so that followed it.

Such was the pattern even among the ancient Greeks, who had had their own dark age from about 1200 to 750 BC, when their earlier "Mycenaean" culture lapsed into illiteracy. The Homeric epics that came next are certainly extraordinary, but they look more like examples of individual genius than of the collective brilliance of a whole culture.[3] We find the first real ensemble of geniuses in the fifth and fourth centuries BC, and even then not scattered all over Greece but centered in the single city of Athens, from the time of Aeschylus to that of Aristotle. A somewhat less dazzling company of geniuses appeared again in the city of Rome in the late Republic and early Empire, again for some 200 years, say from the time of Cicero to that of Tacitus. After that, to find anything truly comparable we must wait for the Italian Renaissance, which occurred largely in Florence and again lasted for about 200 years, say from the time of Dante to that of Machiavelli. Intriguingly, the golden ages of Athens, Rome, and Florence produced not only great thought and literature but also comparably brilliant art and architecture.

Besides those three great cultural communities that achieved brilliance, we can find other, smaller sparks, some of them just individual geniuses. My own research on the Byzantine historians includes five brilliant writers from different periods.[4] None of them knew each other personally, though Michael Psellus seems to have died only a few years before Anna Comnena was born, and Anna seems to have died only a few years before the birth of Nicetas Choniates. These five masters were however only the most talented representatives of a great tradition: over 120 historians, roughly one for every decade of Byzantine history, who continued a long line of Greek historians going back to Herodotus. Most Byzantine historians were wealthy and well educated, and benefited from writing their works in Constantinople, which for most of the Byzantine period was the greatest cultural, political, and economic center of the Western world. The Byzantines also produced some significant works of theology, poetry, hagiography, philosophy, and scholarship, to the point where we can think of Byzantium as having a resilient though somewhat attenuated cultural community that lasted twelve centuries.

Byzantine culture was hardly inferior to the culture of the Greeks during the six centuries after their golden age ended around 300 BC. During that "Hellenistic" period, the Greeks produced many authors who were good but not great—along with an occasional genius like Theocritus, Polybius, Plutarch, or Longus—as well as notable mathematicians and scientists, who followed a rather different pattern of development from writers or artists. Western civilization has been producing occasional literary and artistic geniuses since the Italian Renaissance, though Western literary achievements have been less consistent than Western scientific progress, which depended on the cumulative efforts of many scientists. We can also identify a few more places and times, like Paris from around 1650 to 1850 or London from around 1750 to 1950, that produced or attracted groups of literary geniuses who deserve comparison with the communities at Athens, Rome, and Florence during their golden ages. Throughout modern times the cultural spark appears now and then, here and there, sometimes dimmer and sometimes brighter. Today we can congratulate ourselves on the state of our scientific knowledge, but not so much on our literature, music, and art. Nobody really knows how to foster cultural brilliance, but contemporary American universities seem not to be very good at it, as Derek Bok of Harvard has implied.[5]

As I have noted, no one to date has fully explained the reasons for the brilliance of Athens in the fifth and fourth centuries BC. In any case, Athenian brilliance was by no means uniform. Today the Golden Age of Athens probably looks more uniformly brilliant than it really was, because most of the mediocre writing has been lost and most of the mediocre buildings have disappeared. Golden ages and their greatest achievements age gracefully; for example, most of us like the Parthenon better without its original bright red, blue, and gold paint. Among the fifth-century Greeks' less happy inventions was something much like postmodernism: the doctrine of the sophists Protagoras and Gorgias, both Greeks who came to Athens from other cities, who argued that nothing has any objective existence and that any opinion is as valid as any other. According to Plato, Socrates refuted such sophistry by observing that it implied any man's opinion about his future health would be as true as that of the best physician.[6] After a fairly short time, the ideas of Protagoras and Gorgias became discredited, and the very different ideas of Socrates and Plato prevailed.

Not surprisingly, communities of geniuses only appear in cities, though not necessarily in large cities. The urban population of Athens in the fifth century was around 35,000, a little larger than today's town of Princeton and just over half the size of today's Palo Alto. Rome had a population of perhaps 250,000 around 1 AD, and Florence's was around 95,000 in 1340 but just 32,000 in 1349, after the Black Death.[7] Being surrounded by geniuses obviously encourages genius and discourages mediocrity, and in fifth-century Athens geniuses certainly learned from each other. The young Thucydides is said to have been moved to tears when he heard Herodotus give a public reading from his *Histories*. The great tragic and comic poets saw each other's plays and competed twice a year for prizes for the best tragedy and comedy. In Plato's *Symposium* a tragic poet, Agathon, celebrates winning the first prize for tragedy by hosting a party attended by Socrates and the comic poet Aristophanes. Such parties involved heavy drinking and no female guests, though flute-girls could be part of the entertainment. In fact, in ancient Greece men looked down on women, aristocrats looked down on commoners, free men looked down on slaves, and all Greeks looked down on foreigners. No one seems to have been bothered by the lack of diversity in race, class, or gender among the largely aristocratic white male geniuses of the time. The ancient Greeks liked individual athletic competitions but not team sports, apparently because they were interested in true brilliance, not in cooperation among athletes of different abilities.

While the Greeks had nothing like our colleges or universities in the fifth century, in the fourth century they founded the first schools that offered a higher education: the Academy of Plato, the Lyceum of Aristotle, the Garden of Epicurus, and the Stoa of Zeno, all of them at Athens, along with the Library and Museum at Greek-speaking

Alexandria in Greek-ruled Egypt. These schools, instead of all teaching similar ideas like most American universities, represented approaches that often differed radically from each other: Platonism, Aristotelianism, Epicureanism, and Stoicism at Athens, and literary and scientific research at Alexandria. Uncomfortably for modern professors, after the foundation of these schools we find less great literature and less original thinking than before, though literary and scientific scholarship continued to progress. One reason for the decline of originality is probably that the schools seldom challenged the ideas they had inherited from their founders. Since Roman schools never developed to the same extent as Greek schools, many Romans received their higher education by attending the schools of Athens. During the Renaissance, Florence intermittently had a university, but it was founded later than several other Italian universities and never became one of the most distinguished among them. Universities are evidently not a prerequisite for cultural brilliance.

At least in the opinion of most ancient authorities, the main reason for the decline of Greek literature and free thought was the loss of Greek political freedom. The extreme democracy of Athens, which was never typical of Greek cities, really functioned only during the fifth and fourth centuries and worked best under the informal leadership of Pericles. After Alexander the Great, the main powers in the Greek world were kings, and Athens was ruled mostly by tyrants. The theory that political liberty fosters great literature and great ideas also fits passably into the history of Rome, where culture thrived in the last years of the Roman Republic, persisted under the relatively benign rule of Augustus, suffered under the more despotic emperors of the first century AD, then revived somewhat under the "Five Good Emperors." Some further confirmation of this theory appears during the Italian Renaissance, which corresponded roughly to the period of the Republic of Florence from 1282 to 1494, before the republic succumbed to a French invasion and a monarchy under the family of its former republican leaders, the Medici. Nonetheless, each of these great cultural communities had political leaders so strong that they often gave their names to the communities: Periclean Athens, Augustan Rome, and Medicean Florence.

Nothing comparable to these great cultural communities seems ever to have existed outside Western culture as broadly defined. Although there have been some individual geniuses and significant cultural communities outside the West, particularly in China and India, Saul Bellow still had a point when he famously inquired in 1994, "Who is the Tolstoy of the Zulus? The Proust of the Papuans?" The answers Bellow received were much more abusive than informative.[8] Recent arguments against the unique brilliance of Western culture have scarcely ever tried to show that groups of authors and works outside Western civilization were of a quality comparable to the great authors and works of the West. Instead we hear a few atypical anecdotes, easily refuted errors and outright lies, irrelevant condemnations of the many immoral things Westerners have done throughout history, indignant demands to respect supposedly oppressed cultures, and postmodernist denunciations of "value judgments" and "positivism." Since the idea that the West has been culturally superior has been attacked only by attacking the idea that any culture could possibly be superior, we may safely assume that Western culture is indeed superior. Even those who claim they disagree almost always rely on Western mathematics, science, and medicine in preference to non-Western alternatives.

Encouraging Brilliance

History may tempt us to think that "diversity" in race, class, and gender is actually a disadvantage in creating a brilliant intellectual community. After all, ancient Athens, ancient Rome, and Renaissance Florence were brilliant and relatively homogeneous, and today's universities have become steadily less brilliant while becoming less homogeneous. Yet most cultures in most periods have been homogeneous but not brilliant, and we have no obvious reason to think that a culture of different races and classes and both genders cannot be brilliant. Athens attracted geniuses from other cities, like Herodotus from Halicarnassus and Aristotle from Stagira; Herodotus and Thucydides may well have been only partly Greek in race, since the name of Herodotus's father Lyxes is Carian and that of Thucydides's father Olorus is Thracian. Athens's geniuses included not just aristocrats like Thucydides and Aristophanes but also men of more modest backgrounds like Euripides and Socrates. The ancient Greeks, despite the inferior position of women in their society, rightly counted Sappho, who lived in Mytilene around 600 BC, as a great poetess. Politics and commerce made Periclean Athens,

Augustan Rome, and Medicean Florence attractive to talented outsiders, and talented people from undistinguished families won fame in all three cities. A mixture of races, classes, and genders seems not in itself to inhibit cultural brilliance.

What does appear to be a distinct disadvantage for cultural brilliance—and for free speech and thought, good literature and art, and sound scholarship—is an obsession with race, class, and gender groups at the expense of an interest in individual talent and in humanity in general. If all that really matters are race, class, and gender groups, their members should avoid distinguishing themselves from their groups or emphasizing what they have in common with the rest of the human race. The result is to discourage thinkers, speakers, and writers from distinguishing themselves by their individuality, originality, or excellence, but rather to encourage them to dedicate themselves to advancing the interests of their race, class, or gender. If they belong to an oppressed group, they should concentrate on their group's oppression and not identify with its oppressors. If they belong to an oppressive group, they should concentrate on trying to atone for their oppression but not presume to understand the oppressed. The leftists in today's universities insist that members of an oppressive group cannot possibly understand what members of an oppressed group endure. Efforts by the oppressive group to understand the culture of the oppressed are "cultural appropriation," while efforts to teach an oppressed group to understand the culture of the oppressors are "cultural imperialism." Such an ideology drastically restricts the scope of debate, teaching, scholarship, literature, and art.

The compulsion to put fighting oppression ahead of everything else might be defensible if women and minorities were being severely and systematically oppressed in America. But America has never been more tolerant of women and minorities than it is now. Problems remain, as they always do, but not problems like the genocide or fanaticism that have led to severe oppression in places like Bosnia, Rwanda, Syria, Afghanistan, or Myanmar, let alone Nazi Germany, the Stalinist Soviet Union, Maoist China, or Cambodia. One proof that oppression is not widespread in America is that so many of the alleged instances of oppression are isolated or trivial. Unprecedented attention to police mistreatment of black suspects in the last few years has turned up only a handful of incidents, in most of which the police behaved justifiably.

Most of the same people who find Donald Trump's exploitation of women intolerable were ready to overlook similar exploitation of women by Bill Clinton. If a significant part of the oppression of minorities is "microaggressions" in things like Halloween costumes and names of athletic teams, that oppression cannot be severe. Most Irish Americans, whose ancestors once suffered severe poverty, abuse, and prejudice in both Ireland and America, now happily tolerate leprechaun costumes and a team called the Fighting Irish. Minorities will never be truly equal members of American society until they judge members of majorities as individuals and refuse to take offense where none is meant. Anyone who tells all whites they are racists is a racist of the worst sort, who condemns people for their race alone.

Especially in America, all of us belong to many minority groups: men, white men, white women, liberals, conservatives, moderates, members of religious and ethnic groups, people of every age group, and so on. Belonging to some of these minorities is to varying degrees a choice; belonging to others is not. Belonging to practically any of these minorities can be a disadvantage in some cases (for example, conservatives in most universities). Outsiders are seldom able to understand exactly what being a member of each minority group is like, unless they have good imaginations or are former members of the group with good memories, like old people who remember what it was like to be young. A major function of great literature and much scholarship is to help us understand what different people are or were like. But serious problems will arise if, for instance, a student who is half-Chinese, half-German, Unitarian, Libertarian, vegetarian, left-handed, one-legged, heterosexual, male, and nineteen years old decides that everyone who fails to share all ten of his adjectives cannot understand him or be understood by him. Such a refusal to understand others will make him unfit to study or teach in a university, to read or do objective scholarship, or to read or write anything of general interest. Objective scholarship, good literature, and good ideas should be accessible to people of all kinds, regardless of the author's group memberships. With a certain amount of effort, readers who are not white, male, or Greek can fully appreciate Herodotus, Aristophanes, and Plato.

What, if anything, can modern universities learn from the intervals of cultural brilliance in Athens, Rome, and Florence, and from occasional cultural brilliance in other times and places? Despite having a far larger population to draw upon than ancient Athens or even the whole ancient Greek world, we cannot realistically hope to have a Sophocles and an Aristophanes in the drama department, a Herodotus and a Thucydides in the history department, a Plato and an Aristotle in the philosophy department, a Phidias and a Praxiteles in the art department, and a Euclid and an Archimedes in the mathematics department. Yet we can hope for universities better than the ones we have now, where men like these would probably never be hired at all because they were elitists, eccentrics, conservatives, disrespectful of academic orthodoxy, too challenging as teachers to get good teaching evaluations, or unable to show that their teaching would make their students more employable.[9] Without eliminating such candidates, our universities should choose their professors carefully, pay them appropriately, and give them job security if they earn it. Our universities should admit students who are interested in ideas and want to learn something. Rather than measuring academic value by racial and sexual "diversity" and refusing to criticize postmodernist, feminist, Marxist, and other leftist orthodoxies, our universities should encourage freedom, excellence, and diversity in thought, teaching, and research. Universities should also trust truly meritocratic systems of hiring and admissions to be fair to women and minorities, and should never hire or admit poorly qualified people simply because of their race, sex, or ideology.

While this much may seem obvious, most of it is far from obvious to the majority of academic administrators and professors today. Overcoming their resistance is a prerequisite for any significant improvement, but they seem to be incapable of reforming themselves under present circumstances. Professors who are already hired probably cannot be dislodged, and even if they could be, under the current system their replacements would probably be even worse and less independent-minded than they are. The time to bring about an improvement in the quality of professors is when new ones are hired, and the only practical means of judging the quality of applicants for professorships is to judge their dissertations, the main basis on which their doctorates are awarded and the foundation of their academic careers. Since the present system judges academic credentials badly, some means of doing it well needs to be created, and a National Dissertation Board is the only means anyone has suggested that is likely to help. A board that the universities had to recognize as qualified would produce judgments that hiring committees and administrators would find hard to ignore. The result would be a gradual but continuous flow of better qualified and more equitably chosen professors into universities and a gradual but continuous improvement in the universities themselves. An Academic Honesty Board should eliminate the worst recent doctorates and the worst current professors (including some with tenure) for reasons that no one who valued honesty could consider illegitimate.

Either alongside these new boards or without them, a newly founded university could provide an example of what most of our current universities could and should be but are not. The new university could offer general courses teaching what every educated person should know, with specialized courses teaching the essentials of each of their subjects. Such a university could encourage genuine freedom of speech and thought and genuine debate about ideas. Postmodernism inevitably discourages competition among ideas, because if all ideas are equally valid, competition among them is pointless. Feminism and Marxism discourage competition among ideas because they condemn their opponents as agents of sexual, racial, and class oppression, regardless of the validity of those opponents' arguments. Yet the majority even of current professors are not orthodox postmodernists, feminists, or Marxists. Most of them are merely indecisive and confused, trying to cope with a bad academic job market, respectful of whatever is in academic fashion, and unwilling, unprepared, or afraid to challenge postmodernism, feminism, or Marxism, at least without having something coherent to put in their place. A new university that was careful to avoid an unreflective and dogmatic conservatism would have a good chance of creating new academic fashions and winning over a growing number of professors and administrators at other universities.

As I have noted, however, the time when these proposals can best be implemented is running out. The quality of graduate dissertations and new professors continues to decline; the number of well-qualified professors trained under an older and better system is steadily decreasing as they leave the profession, retire, or die; and the number of distinguished retired professors who could serve on dissertation or academic honesty boards or could plan a new university is also shrinking as they become inactive or die. As of now, I believe that enough distinguished professors could be found to staff both the dissertation and honesty boards and the faculty of a new university. Yet this may not still be true twenty years from now. With each passing year, these reforms are likely to become a little harder to introduce. Even if the need for such reforms becomes increasingly evident as our universities become ever more glaringly biased and dysfunctional, finding qualified members for dissertation and academic honesty boards would become more difficult, and any new university would find hiring 1,000 outstanding professors harder, even with enough money and determination. Even if postmodernism, Marxism, feminism, and other such ideologies should become generally discredited, as seems already to have begun to happen, this alone would not produce better-trained professors and graduate students. The situation would still not be hopeless—even the worst dark ages eventually come to an end—but any improvements would be smaller and slower than they could be now.

Today the largely unspoken but widely shared assumption is that higher education is incompatible with conservatism. That assumption is patently false. In fact, most of what passes for "innovative" scholarship today is postmodernist drivel, which disregards the rules of evidence and argument and simply applies to one topic after another the same stale theoretical boilerplate that has been mindlessly repeated for more than fifty years.[10] While of course universities should discover new facts and introduce new ideas, the great bulk of what they teach consists of writings, ideas, and events that date from earlier times, often from much earlier times. Even in the sciences and mathematics, the results of very recent research almost always remain uncertain until they have been tested and discussed over a period of years, and many fundamental scientific and mathematical principles are centuries old. Scholarship in the humanities and social sciences also builds on sound contributions by earlier scholars, unless it invokes postmodernism to dismiss those contributions on the ground that nothing can be objectively true. Although some creative works written recently may one day take their place as part of the world's great literature, most of the greatest poems, plays, novels, and essays written thus far go back centuries or millennia. Education must be primarily the study of the past.

The liberal tendency to think that whatever is most recent is best, if carried to its logical conclusion, would mean dismissing as inferior almost all of what higher education has to teach, certainly including most of history, literature, philosophy, and religion as we know them. The main reason that most liberals feel compelled to take postmodernism, Marxism, and feminism so seriously is merely that they are recent. Scholars with any awareness of the past know that postmodernism, Marxism, and feminism developed from earlier ideas at specific times and at some point will go out of style. Historians, economists, and political scientists may well conclude that Marxism has already been refuted by the events of the twentieth century, and philosophers may well conclude that postmodernism has practically refuted itself from the beginning. There is something inherently conservative, in the strict sense though not necessarily in a political sense, about believing that important things can be learned from the past and that those important things should be taught in a university.

Even liberals would have conceded this much until the sixties, when I went to college. By then, after a vast expansion of higher education, many students had no idea what they were doing at college except that their parents wanted them to go, while a few students had radical ideas of what they were doing at college that came from their radical parents. This mix might not have led to widespread student protests without the fear inspired by a combination of the Vietnam War, the military draft, and student deferments that were supposed to be only temporary. The result was a barely coherent student protest movement, consistently antiwar and vaguely against any form of rigor in education. Even this movement would probably not have led to much change in universities if overwhelmingly liberal (though not yet radical) faculties and administrations had not already begun to lose faith in what they were teaching. When students complained that the curriculum they were taught was not "relevant," meaning that it had no obvious relation to their concerns with not being drafted, having fun in college, and deciding what they wanted to do with their lives, most professors and administrators were inclined to think that the curriculum did need updating, at least to the extent of replacing the *Odyssey* with Joyce's *Ulysses* on reading lists and taking a serious look at Marx and Foucault.

One sign of the profound confusion that prevailed in the sixties and seventies among students, faculty, and administrators was that so many students stopped going to class, called this a "strike," and thereby intimidated the faculty and administration into accepting at least some of their demands. When I was a Harvard undergraduate, the students' "strike" turned into a giant party with rock music blaring and marijuana smoke wafting through Harvard Yard. A friend of mine remarked of student strikes, "The university should hire strikebreakers to go to class. That would show the absurdity of the whole thing." Yet almost everyone seemed to accept that studying was a worthless chore that got in the way of the real business of having fun at college—or at any rate of investigating the meaning of life there—and that the only reason to study was to prevent retaliation by parents and professors, who for some ill-defined purposes of their own wanted students to study. These ideas made about as much sense as another idea often heard at the time, that the Vietnam War had been conceived by the older generation as a means of dominating the younger generation and killing some of them off, again for a purpose never made entirely clear. The more politically aware students chanted, "Ho, Ho, Ho Chi Minh! The NLF is gonna win!" With the help of such students, the Communist National Liberation Front did conquer South Vietnam, and together with its Cambodian and Laotian allies drove out or murdered a large part of the population of Indochina.

Today, after the demise of Communism more or less everywhere but North Korea, we can easily forget that in the sixties and seventies many intellectuals, including many non-Marxists, considered its triumph inevitable. An evocative joke after the fall of South Vietnam went, "The optimists are learning Russian; the pessimists are learning Chinese." On a visit during the seventies to an old family friend, the conservative philosopher of history Karl August Wittfogel, I let slip my opinion that the Catholic Church would outlast Communist rule in Eastern Europe. Wittfogel exploded, "Much as I hate the Marxists, they are better historians than you!" If one believed Marxism had correctly interpreted the course of history and was certain to triumph, one had to take it very seriously. Although hardly anybody believes in the inexorable triumph of Marxism any more, intellectuals and especially professors have been surprisingly slow to accept the implications of its failure. This is perhaps no stranger than the refusal of the pagan professors of Late Antiquity to accept the failure of paganism as late as the sixth century, long after the great majority of the Roman population had become Christian. One reason for wanting a new university is that it might finally convince some professors at the old universities that Marxism has failed and that something different might be the wave of the future. If Communism could collapse under the weight of its own failings and some firm opposition, surely campus leftism can do the same.

While moderate liberalism is compatible with a coherent higher education—even if liberals may offer it with less conviction than conservatives—a coherent higher education is very nearly incompatible with the radical egalitarianism of the most influential American professors today. The radical democracy of Athens, which chose its officials by lot, was always suspicious of the city's geniuses, who were often suspected of having aristocratic sympathies because they believed in excellence of all kinds. For such reasons the Athenian democracy fined Aristophanes, exiled Thucydides, and executed Socrates. If egalitarianism is the overriding principle, then preferring the best ideas, assigning the best books, admitting the best students, and hiring the best professors is "elitist" and discriminatory. On the other hand, even the most zealous egalitarians are reluctant to argue explicitly for preferring mediocre ideas, assigning mediocre books, admitting mediocre students, and hiring mediocre professors in the interest of equality. Egalitarians would rather argue that every idea, book, and applicant is as good as any other—or, better yet, that we should hire professors who put egalitarianism first, so that they can propound ideas, assign books, admit students, and hire other professors to help groups that have not been treated equally in the past because of race, class, or gender. The results of such a program are the mediocre curricula, faculties, and student bodies of most American colleges and universities today. If someone has better ideas for improving them than judging professors by the quality of their work or founding a new university dedicated to excellence, the time to share those ideas is now.

REFERENCES

Andreescu-Treadgold, Irina, and Warren Treadgold. "Procopius and the Imperial Panels of San Vitale." *Art Bulletin* 79 (1997): 708–23.

Arreola, Raoul A. *Developing a Comprehensive Faculty Evaluation System: A Guide to Designing, Building, and Operating Large-Scale Faculty Evaluation Systems.* Bolton, MA: Anker, 2007.

Arum, Richard, and Josipa Roksa. *Academically Adrift: Limited Learning on College Campuses.* Chicago: University of Chicago Press, 2011.

Bennett, William J., and David Wilezol. *Is College Worth It?* Nashville: Thomas Nelson, 2013.

Bilgrami, Akeel, and Jonathan R. Cole, eds. *Who's Afraid of Academic Freedom?* New York: Columbia University Press, 2015.

Bok, Derek. *Higher Education in America.* Princeton, NJ: Princeton University Press, 2013.

Brint, Steven. "Focus on the Classroom: Movements to Reform College Teaching and Learning, 1980–2008." In Hermanowicz, *American Academic Profession,* 44–91.

Cole, Jonathan R., Stephen Cole, and Christian C. Weiss. "Academic Freedom: A Pilot Study of Faculty Views," in Bilgrami and Cole, *Who's Afraid,* 343–94.

Douglas, George H. *Education Without Impact: How Our Universities Fail the Young.* New York: Birch Lane Press, 1992.

Douthat, Ross Gregory. *Privilege: Harvard and the Education of the Ruling Class.* New York: Hachette, 2005.

Eagleton, Terry. *After Theory.* New York: Basic Books, 2003.

Feldman, Kenneth A. "Research Productivity and Scholarly Accomplishment of College Teachers as Related to Their Instructional Effectiveness: A Review and Exploration." *Research in Higher Education* 26 (1987): 227–98.

Ferrall, Victor E., Jr. *Liberal Arts at the Brink*. Cambridge, MA: Harvard University Press, 2011.

Fichtenbaum, Rudy. "Why Is US Higher Education in Decline?" *Academe* 99, no. 6 (November–December 2013): 48.

Geiger, Roger L. "Optimizing Research and Teaching: The Bifurcation of Faculty Roles at Research Universities." In Hermanowicz, *American Academic Profession*, 21–43.

Ginsberg, Benjamin. *The Fall of the Faculty: The Rise of the All-Administrative University and Why It Matters*. Oxford: Oxford University Press, 2011.

Grigsby, Mary. *College Life Through the Eyes of Students*. Albany, NY: SUNY Press, 2009.

Hacker, Andrew, and Claudia Dreifus. *Higher Education? How Colleges Are Wasting Our Money and Failing Our Kids—and What We Can Do About It*. New York: Times Books, 2010.

Hanson, Victor Davis, John Heath, and Bruce Thornton. *Bonfire of the Humanities: Rescuing the Classics in an Impoverished Age*. Wilmington, DE: ISI Books, 2001.

Hart, Jeffrey. *Smiling Through the Cultural Catastrophe: Toward the Revival of Higher Education*. New Haven, CT: Yale University Press, 2001.

Hermanowicz, Joseph C., ed. *The American Academic Profession: Transformation in Contemporary Higher Education*. Baltimore, MD: Johns Hopkins University Press, 2011.

Horowitz, David, and Jacob Laksin. *One-Party Classroom: How Radical Professors at America's Top Colleges Indoctrinate Students and Undermine Our Democracy*. New York: Crown Forum, 2009.

Jencks, Christopher, and David Riesman. *The Academic Revolution*. With a new foreword by Martin Trow. Chicago: University of Chicago, 1977. First published 1968.

Karabell, Zachary. *What's College For? The Struggle to Define American Higher Education*. New York: Basic Books, 1998.

Keller, Morton, and Phyllis Keller. *Making Harvard Modern: The Rise of America's University*. New York: Oxford University Press, 2001.

Keeling, Richard P., and Richard H. Hersh. *We're Losing Our Minds: Rethinking American Higher Education*. New York: Palgrave Macmillan, 2011.

Lamont, Michèle. *How Professors Think: Inside the Curious World of Academic Judgment*. Cambridge, MA: Harvard University Press, 2009.

Lederman, Doug. "Studies Challenge the Findings of 'Academically Adrift.'" *Inside Higher Ed*, May 20, 2013. https://www.insidehighered.com/news/2013/05/20/studies-challenge-findings-academically-adrift.

Lewis, Harry R. *Excellence Without a Soul: How a Great University Forgot Education*. New York: PublicAffairs, 2006.

Lewis, Lionel S. *Marginal Worth: Teaching and the Academic Labor Market*. New Brunswick, NJ: Transaction Publishers, 1996.

London, Herbert I. *Decline and Revival in Higher Education*. New Brunswick, NJ: Transaction Publishers, 2010.

Mahler, Jonathan. "The Thinker." *New York Times Magazine*, September 19, 2008. http://www.nytimes.com/2008/09/21/magazine/21jolley-t.html.

Menand, Louis. *The Marketplace of Ideas: Reform and Resistance in the American University*. New York: W.W. Norton, 2010.

Moss, Mark. *Education and Its Discontents: Teaching, the Humanities, and the Importance of a Liberal Education in the Age of Mass Information*. Lanham, MD: Rowman & Littlefield, 2012.

Naftulin, Donald H., John E. Ware Jr., and Frank A. Donnelly. "The Doctor Fox Lecture: A Paradigm of Educational Seduction." *Journal of Medical Education* 48 (1973): 630–5.

Ober, Josiah. "Letter from the President: Too Much Companionship?" *American Philological Association Newsletter* 32 (2009): 1–3.

Professor X. *In the Basement of the Ivory Tower: Confessions of an Accidental Academic*. New York: Viking, 2011.

Rosovsky, Henry. *The University: An Owner's Manual*. New York: Norton, 1990.

Shields, Jon A., and Joshua M. Dunn Sr. *Passing on the Right: Conservative Professors in the Progressive University*. Oxford: Oxford University Press, 2016.

Shweder, Richard A. "To Follow the Argument Where It Leads: An Antiquarian View of the Aim of Academic Freedom at the University of Chicago." In Bilgrami and Cole, *Who's Afraid*, 190–238.

Slaughter, Sheila. "Academic Freedom, Professional Autonomy, and the State." In Hermanowicz, *American Academic Profession*, 241–73.

Sokal, Alan. *Beyond the Hoax: Science, Philosophy and Culture.* Oxford: Oxford University Press, 2008.

Taylor, Mark C. *Crisis on Campus: A Bold Plan for Reforming Our Colleges and Universities.* New York: Alfred A. Knopf, 2010.

Treadgold, Warren. "Imaginary Early Christianity." *International History Review* 15 (1993): 535–45.

———. "Predicting the Accession of Theodosius I." *Mediterraneo Antico* 8 (2005): 767–91.

———. "Taking Sources on Their Own Terms and on Ours: Peter Brown's Late Antiquity." *Antiquité Tardive* 2 (1994): 153–9.

Trow, Martin. *Twentieth-Century Higher Education: Elite to Mass to Universal.* Edited by Michael Burrage. Baltimore, MD: Johns Hopkins University Press, 2010.

Vedder, Richard Kent. *Going Broke by Degree: Why College Costs Too Much.* Washington, D.C.: AEI Press, 2004.

Verene, Donald Phillip. "Does Online Education Rest on a Mistake?" *Academic Questions* 26, no. 3 (2013): 296–307.

Wickham, Chris. *Framing the Early Middle Ages: Europe and the Mediterranean, 400–800.* Oxford: Oxford University Press, 2005.

Yancey, George. *Compromising Scholarship: Religious and Political Bias in American Higher Education.* Waco, TX: Baylor University Press, 2011.

NOTES

CHAPTER 1: DO UNIVERSITIES MATTER?

1 http://www.gallup.com/poll/1669/General-Mood-Country.aspx. The lowest level of dissatisfaction during Obama's presidency was 62 percent, in 2009. Polls on the "direction of the country" (reflecting opinions about the near future rather than the present), though somewhat less pessimistic, were still consistently negative throughout Obama's presidency; see http://www.realclearpolitics.com/epolls/other/direction_of_country-902.html.

2 Trump won the votes of 67 percent of whites without a college degree but only 49 percent of white college graduates, according to a *New York Times* exit poll (https://www.nytimes.com/interactive/2016/11/08/us/politics/election-exit-polls.html).

3 The same poll showed that only 19 percent of Democrats and Democratic sympathizers held this view. Since 62 percent of Republicans think that colleges prepare their students relatively well for the workforce, the Republicans' objection seems to be to the colleges' ideology rather than to their effectiveness. See Hannah Fingerhut, "Republicans Skeptical of Colleges' Impact on U.S., but Most See Benefits for Workforce Preparation," Pew Research Center, July 20, 2017 (http://www.pewresearch.org/fact-tank/2017/07/20/republicans-skeptical-of-colleges-impact-on-u-s-but-most-see-benefits-for-workforce-preparation/).

4 This view is even held by 55 percent of Democrats (though some of them may think that universities present too few leftist viewpoints). See Cato Institute/YouGov, "Cato Institute 2017 Free Speech and Tolerance Survey," August 15–23, 2017, p. 30, question 46 (https://object.cato.org/sites/cato.org/files/survey-reports/topline/cato-free-speech-tolerance-toplines.pdf).

5 This conclusion is not really controversial among people familiar with American universities. The most systematic demonstration is in George Yancey, *Compromising Scholarship: Religious and Political Bias in American Higher Education* (Waco, TX: Baylor University Press, 2011). For two more recent surveys, see Sandra Kotta (an obvious pseudonym), "Bald Men Fighting Over a Comb: Arguments About the Classical Tradition," *Quillette*, May 17, 2017 (http://quillette.com/2017/05/17/bald-men-fighting-comb-arguments-classical-tradition/); and Uri Harris, "Are the Social Sciences Undergoing a Purity Spiral?" *Quillette*, July 6, 2017 (http://quillette.com/2017/07/06/social-sciences-undergoing-purity-spiral/).

6 Their dislike of Trump mainly derives from his disdain for factual accuracy, political expertise, and ideological coherence, all of which are important to most conservative intellectuals (though not to postmodernists).

7 This institution, Berea College, is likely to be harmed by the tax a good deal more than Harvard, Princeton, Yale, or Stanford are. Erica L. Green, "A Tuition-Free College Takes a Hit," *New York Times*, December 21, 2017, A18.

8 Trump, of course, was elected in 2016 with no political experience at all; but he claimed, as Obama did not, that his lack of political experience was an advantage.

9 See http://www.realclearpolitics.com/epolls/other/president_obama_job_approval-1044.html.

10 Buckley was right about the trend, though conservatives and moderates who read his book today will be struck by how much less serious the ideological imbalance was in his time.

11 Cf. Frank Bruni, "College's Priceless Value," *New York Times*, February 11, 2015, A27, and "College, Poetry, and Purpose," *New York Times*, February 18, 2015, A21. Note that Bruni's evidently brilliant teacher with a respectable publishing record, Anne Drury Hall, now holds only the rank of lecturer, not professor, at the University of Pennsylvania.

12 See Foundation for Individual Rights in Education (FIRE), "Bias Response Team Report 2017" (https://www.thefire.org/fire-guides/report-on-bias-reporting-systems-2017/).

13 Of the others, fifty identified themselves as Independents, while the rest "identified themselves with some other political party or refused to respond to the question." See Jonathan R. Cole, Stephen Cole, and Christian C. Weiss, "Academic Freedom: A Pilot Study of Faculty Views," in *Who's Afraid of Academic Freedom?*, ed. Akeel Bilgrami and Jonathan R. Cole (New York: Columbia University Press, 2015), 347–9.

14 Cole, Cole, and Weiss, "Academic Freedom," 365–6.

15 A failure to recognize the lack of impact of silenced conservative and moderate professors is one of several serious problems with Jon A. Shields and Joshua M. Dunn Sr., *Passing on the Right: Conservative Professors in the Progressive University* (Oxford: Oxford University Press, 2016), which puts a half-heartedly optimistic construction on the thoroughly alarming facts.

16 See http://inclusion.uchicago.edu/ and https://csl.uchicago.edu/get-help/bias-response-team on the university's own website. Cf. Richard A. Shweder, "To Follow the Argument Where It Leads: An Antiquarian View of the Aim of Academic Freedom at the University of Chicago," in Bilgrami and Cole, *Who's Afraid*, 190–238, especially 200, where he cites a Chicago professor who in addressing a graduating class "essentially argued . . . that the ardor and fearlessness of scholars to follow the argument where it leads and the robustness of the tradition of free thinking within university environments are NOT [capitals in original] best protected by separating thought from well-intentioned social action. Such is the contemporary state of intellectual play at the University of Chicago."

17 For a case in point at "Catholic" Marquette University, see George Will, "Academic Freedom Goes On Trial," *Washington Post*, December 30, 2017

(https://www.washingtonpost.com/opinions/academic-freedom-goes-on-trial/2017/12/29/81cb9268-ebf6-11e7-9f92-10a2203f6c8d_story.html).

CHAPTER 2: THE PROBLEMS

1 The National Center for Education Statistics (https://nces.ed.gov/fastfacts/display.asp?id=76) estimated average annual college expenses in 2014–15 at $18,632 for public four-year institutions and at $37,990 for private four-year institutions, amounts that will surely increase for 2017–18 and thereafter.

2 See the tuition figures at https://www.usnews.com/best-colleges/rankings/national-universities, ranging from $45,320 a year at Princeton to $49,480 a year at Yale, amounts that again will surely increase over the next four years. The out-of-state tuition at the University of California at Berkeley ($40,191) is not much less. On these five universities and their endowments, see pp. 119–20 above.

3 See "5 Things To Consider When Refinancing Student Loans," *Make Lemonade* (https://www.makelemonade.co/top-reads/refinancing-student-loans-5-things).

4 Refreshingly, the former president of Harvard, Derek Bok, *Higher Education in America* (Princeton, NJ: Princeton University Press, 2013), 3, concedes that probably American universities' "impressive standing in the world owes less to the success of our own system than it does to the weakness of foreign universities."

5 For the 2011 figures, compiled by the American Association of University Professors (AAUP), see https://www.aaup.org/sites/default/files/Faculty_Trends_0.pdf. Cf. Victor E. Ferrall Jr., *Liberal Arts at the Brink* (Cambridge, MA: Harvard University Press, 2011), 144. To take another measure, the credit hours taught by regular faculty in public research universities fell from about 55 percent in 1992 to about 40 percent in 2006; see Roger L. Geiger, "Optimizing Research and Teaching: The Bifurcation of Faculty Roles at Research Universities," in *The American Academic Profession: Transformation in Contemporary Higher Education*, ed. Joseph C. Hermanowicz (Baltimore, MD: Johns Hopkins University Press, 2011), 37.

6 SHEEO, "State Higher Education Finance FY 2012: A Project of the Staff of the State Higher Education Executive Officers (SHEEO)," 2013, p. 24, table 3, http://www.sheeo.org/sites/default/files/publications/SHEF-FY12.pdf.

7 Andrew Hacker and Claudia Dreifus, *Higher Education? How Colleges Are Wasting Our Money and Failing Our Kids—and What We Can Do About It* (New York: Times Books, 2010), 28.

8 Rudy Fichtenbaum, "Why Is US Higher Education in Decline?," *Academe* 99, no. 6 (November–December 2013), 48.

9 The result of a survey sponsored by *TIME* magazine and the Carnegie Corporation of New York: Josh Sanburn, "Higher-Education Poll," *TIME*, October 18, 2012, http://nation.time.com/2012/10/18/higher-education-poll.

10 Harry R. Lewis, *Excellence Without a Soul: How a Great University Forgot Education* (New York: PublicAffairs, 2006), 18.

11 Richard Arum and Josipa Roksa, *Academically Adrift: Limited Learning on College Campuses* (Chicago: University of Chicago Press, 2011), 35–6 and 56. For weak objections to these findings and convincing defenses of them, see Doug

Lederman, "Studies Challenge the Findings of 'Academically Adrift,'" *Inside Higher Ed*, May 20, 2013 (https://www.insidehighered.com/news/2013/05/20/ studies-challenge-findings-academically-adrift).

12 Bok, *Higher Education*, 179–80.

13 Arum and Roksa, *Academically Adrift*, 97 and 100.

14 Bok, *Higher Education*, 183.

15 Among several studies that have reached more or less the same conclusions, see especially Mary Grigsby, *College Life Through the Eyes of Students* (Albany, NY: SUNY Press, 2009).

16 Arum and Roksa, *Academically Adrift*, 76–7.

17 Bok, *Higher Education*, 85–6.

18 Bok, *Higher Education*, 88 (four-year colleges), 102 (two-year colleges), and 104 (for-profit colleges).

19 Louis Menand, *The Marketplace of Ideas: Reform and Resistance in the American University* (New York: W.W. Norton, 2010), 88.

20 Lewis, *Excellence*, 58.

21 Ross Gregory Douthat, *Privilege: Harvard and the Education of the Ruling Class* (New York: Hachette, 2005), 133.

22 Jeffrey Hart, *Smiling Through the Cultural Catastrophe: Toward the Revival of Higher Education* (New Haven, CT: Yale University Press, 2001), 247.

23 Cf. the remarks of Morton Keller and Phyllis Keller, *Making Harvard Modern: The Rise of America's University* (New York: Oxford University Press, 2001), 353–5, who say of Harvard what is even more applicable to many other institutions (they mention the Universities of Michigan and Wisconsin): "Over time, the political correctness of the 1970s and 1980s lost its confrontational edge. By the end of the century it had become a pervasive liberal orthodoxy." Some particularly egregious examples of leftist courses are discussed in David Horowitz and Jacob Laksin, *One-Party Classroom: How Radical Professors at America's Top Colleges Indoctrinate Students and Undermine Our Democracy* (New York: Crown Forum, 2009).

24 Keller and Keller, *Making Harvard Modern*, 490.

25 Bok, *Higher Education*, 370.

26 Menand, *Marketplace*, 155.

27 Terry Eagleton, *After Theory* (New York: Basic Books, 2003), 13n1.

28 Tamar Lewin, "Interest Fading in Humanities, Colleges Worry," *New York Times*, October 31, 2013, A1.

29 Steven Brint, "Focus on the Classroom: Movements to Reform College Teaching and Learning, 1980–2008," in Hermanowicz, *American Academic Profession*, 46.

30 Brint, "Focus," 79.

31 Bok, *Higher Education*, 228.

32 Jon Marcus, "University Enrollment Decline Continues into Sixth Straight Year," *The Hechinger Report*, December 20, 2017 (http://hechingerreport.org/ university-enrollment-decline-continues-into-sixth-straight-year/).

33 Menand, *Marketplace*, 152.

34 "How Science Goes Wrong," *Economist*, October 19, 2013, 13. See also above, pp. 90–1.

35 Nabokov actually had quite a bit of trouble with the academic job market in his day. See his academic novel *Pnin* (1957), set at a lightly fictionalized Cornell.

36 See pp. 82–7 above on academic publications.

37 See pp. 55–61 above on teaching.

38 See Jonathan Mahler, "The Thinker," *New York Times Magazine*, September 19, 2008 (http://www.nytimes.com/2008/09/21/magazine/21jolley-t.html).

39 After the Auburn administration found that its philosophy department came first in its internal ranking of departments, it changed its criteria, and then, when philosophy came first again, "decided to give up on the rankings altogether" (Mahler, "Thinker").

40 Richard Kent Vedder, *Going Broke by Degree: Why College Costs Too Much* (Washington, D.C.: AEI Press, 2004), 60–4, tries to challenge this widely accepted conclusion by concentrating on salaries for senior faculty in four-year private institutions, emphasizing that the sharpest fall in salaries occurred in the 1970s, and citing opportunities for professors to earn outside income and "the rising workforce participation of spouses." None of this alters the fact that average faculty salaries have not increased significantly since 1970, though some professors have of course done better than average, taken second jobs, or married rich.

41 Benjamin Ginsberg, *The Fall of the Faculty: The Rise of the All-Administrative University and Why It Matters* (Oxford: Oxford University Press, 2011), 24–5 with table 2.

42 The classic study is Ginsberg, *Fall*, which gives an excellent account of administrators, though I think it depicts the faculty too sympathetically.

43 Jay P. Greene, Brian Kisida, and Jonathan Mills, "Administrative Bloat at American Universities: The Real Reason for High Costs in Higher Education," Goldwater Institute Policy Report no. 239, August 17, 2010 (https://goldwaterinstitute.org/wp-content/uploads/cms_page_media/2015/3/24/Administrative%20Bloat.pdf). See also pp. 111–15 above.

44 See Lewis, *Excellence*, 155, on the new beer pub in Harvard Yard, where the only dormitories are for freshmen, practically all of whom are two or three years younger than the legal drinking age.

45 Cf. Mark Moss, *Education and Its Discontents: Teaching, the Humanities, and the Importance of a Liberal Education in the Age of Mass Information* (Lanham, MD: Rowman & Littlefield, 2012), 137.

46 Moss, *Education*, 167.

47 Lewis, *Excellence*, 265.

48 Richard P. Keeling and Richard H. Hersh, *We're Losing Our Minds: Rethinking American Higher Education* (New York: Palgrave Macmillan, 2011), 176.

49 Arum and Roksa, *Academically Adrift*, 144.

50 Bok, *Higher Education*, 358.

51 Bok, *Higher Education*, 407.

52 On proposals for the abolition of tenure, see pp. 77–82 above.

53 Michael D. Shear, "With Website to Research Colleges, Obama Abandons Ranking System," *New York Times*, September 13, 2015, A31.

54 See pp. 115–16 above.

55 Robert C. Koons, "Campus Chaos, and How to Fix It," *American Greatness*, June 19, 2017 (https://amgreatness.com/2017/06/19/campus-chaos-fix/).

56 See p. 19 above.

57 William J. Bennett and David Wilezol, *Is College Worth It?* (Nashville: Thomas Nelson, 2013), 182–3.

58 See Edward F. Robinson and John A. Williams, "Academic Freedom and Tenure: Hillsdale College, Michigan," *Academe: Bulletin of the AAUP* (May–June 1988), 29–33.

59 See the NAS website at www.nas.org/about/overview.

60 See the recent remarks of one of the founders of the NAS, Herbert I. London, in London, *Decline and Revival in Higher Education* (New Brunswick, NJ: Transaction Publishers, 2010), vi ("In some sense, this is a tale of despair, since I believe the academy predicated on the free exchange of opinion has been transmogrified into a center for orthodoxies") and 6–8 (a more detailed description of the problems as he sees them).

61 See its website at https://heterodoxacademy.org/. (Again, I am a member.) FIRE does some excellent work but is not an organization of professors. See its website at https://www.thefire.org/.

62 Ronald Brownstein, "Why There's Doubt About a College Education: Whites Are More Dubious Than Minorities That a College Degree Puts Graduates on the Path to Success," *National Journal*, November 7, 2013.

63 See Julian Zorthian, "Americans Are Divided Over Whether College Degrees Are Worth It," *Fortune*, September 7, 2017 (http://fortune.com/2017/09/07/americans-college-worth-it/).

64 Sandy Baum, Jennifer Ma, and Kathleen Payea, "Education Pays 2013," College Board, 2013, http://trends.collegeboard.org/sites/default/files/education-pays-2013-full-report.pdf.

65 "Is College Worth It?" *Economist*, April 5, 2014, 23–4.

CHAPTER 3: THE ORIGINS OF CAMPUS LEFTISM

1 Though one can certainly find many features of these ideas in the works of Herbert Marcuse, Michel Foucault, Noam Chomsky, Paul Goodman, and various other writers, none of them truly founded or formulated this movement in the form it has now taken. It is a more spontaneous growth than Marxism, postmodernism, and most other recent ideologies.

2 Though in Britain Jeremy Corbyn is a more orthodox socialist, most of his student admirers are much less orthodox.

3 Everyone on the bus that took me to and from my military physical examination at the Boston Navy Yard in 1970 failed it except for one (not me), who passed only after he told the examiners he wanted to volunteer. My Harvard class was 1971, and according to the plaque in Harvard's Memorial Church, not one Harvard man from a class later than 1968 died in Vietnam. (A total of twenty-two Harvard men died there.)

4 Such was the thesis of Martin Bernal's *Black Athena: Afroasiatic Roots of Classical Civilization*, 3 vols. (New Brunswick, NJ: Rutgers University Press, 1987, 1991, and 2006), easily refuted by Mary Lefkowitz, *Not Out of Africa: How "Afrocentrism" Became an Excuse to Teach Myth As History* (New York: Basic

Books, 1996), and others. Since Bernal's followers thought facts were irrelevant, they ignored the refutations.

CHAPTER 4: WHAT IS GOOD TEACHING?

1 The next year I was nominated again and agreed to be considered after the selection process was changed to have department chairmen ask for references from two graduate advisees from lists of five advisees provided by the nominees. I did not receive the award.

2 For some reason, the last time I checked the site, my own generally positive ratings—which I am pleased to say included a chili pepper—had disappeared.

3 Lewis, *Excellence*, 83.

4 Raoul A. Arreola, *Developing a Comprehensive Faculty Evaluation System: A Guide to Designing, Building, and Operating Large-Scale Faculty Evaluation Systems* (Bolton, MA: Anker, 2007), 101–2.

5 See National Center for Education Statistics, *Digest of Education Statistics: 2011*, 2012, http://nces.ed.gov/programs/digest/d11/tables/dt11_348.asp. Note that between 1965 and 2009 GRE verbal scores declined from 530 to 456, while quantitative scores rose from 533 to 590. During the same period, GRE scores rose from 617 to 650 in biology and from 628 to 699 in chemistry, while scores in literature fell from 591 to 541.

6 For these three suggestions, see Hacker and Dreifus, *Higher Education?*, 88. Cf. Moss, *Education*, 150: "Anyone who has been teaching or in a lecture hall or classroom has seen the students on Facebook or surfing the net during a teacher's lesson or a professor's lecture."

7 For the view that grade inflation is "not very important," see Lewis, *Excellence*, 125–46.

8 See Michael J. Carter and Patricia Y. Lara, "Grade Inflation in Higher Education: Is the End in Sight?" National Association of Scholars, October 11, 2016 (https://www.nas.org/articles/grade_inflation_in_higher_education_is_ the_end_in_sight?utm_source): "There presently is no consensus regarding what should be done about the problems grade inflation has created in higher education, and it is doubtful if such a consensus will ever be reached."

9 Lewis, *Excellence*, 145.

10 By contrast, submitting papers or problem sets online, rather than in class, is perfectly feasible, though it can result in lower class attendance.

11 Eric Bettinger and Susanna Loeb, "Promises and Pitfalls of Online Education," Brookings Report, June 9, 2017 (https://www.brookings.edu/research/promises-and-pitfalls-of-online-education/). Astonishingly, the authors conclude, "The current negative effect of online course taking relative to in-person course taking should not necessarily lead to the conclusion that online courses should be discouraged.... [Rather] the tremendous scale and consistently negative effects of current [online] offerings points [*sic*] to the need to improve these courses." The clear conclusion to be drawn from the results is however not that the content of the online courses was worse than that of the in-person courses, since the two were virtually the same, but that online courses are *inherently* worse than in-person courses.

12 E.g., see Roger Yu, "DeVry to Pay $49M to Students for Misleading Ads," *USA*

Today, July 5, 2017 (https://www.usatoday.com/story/money/2017/07/05/devry-pay-49-m-students-misleading-ads/452189001/).

13 See Tamar Lewin, "After Setbacks, Online Courses Are Rethought: Classes of Thousands, Few of Whom Finish," *New York Times*, December 11, 2013, 1. See also Donald Phillip Verene, "Does Online Education Rest on a Mistake?," *Academic Questions* 26, no. 3 (2013): 296–307.

14 Donald H. Naftulin, John E. Ware Jr., and Frank A. Donnelly, "The Doctor Fox Lecture: A Paradigm of Educational Seduction," *Journal of Medical Education* 48 (1973): 630–5.

15 Christopher Jencks and David Riesman, *The Academic Revolution*, with a new foreword by Martin Trow (Chicago: University of Chicago, 1977; first published 1968), 524.

16 Jencks and Riesman, *Academic Revolution*, 532.

17 Bok, *Higher Education*, 332.

18 Kenneth A. Feldman, "Research Productivity and Scholarly Accomplishment of College Teachers as Related to Their Instructional Effectiveness: A Review and Exploration," *Research in Higher Education* 26 (1987): 240 and 242–4.

19 Naturally in such courses the professor should still take care in reading, grading, and commenting on the students' reports and papers.

CHAPTER 5: WHAT IS GOOD RESEARCH?

1 The best overall study is Ginsberg, *Fall*.

2 The critics whom Biondi penalized (I was not one) received their raises after Biondi's resignation.

3 The Center for Byzantine Studies was abolished and its faculty dispersed around 1980. (Perhaps I should mention that I married one of the dismissed Byzantine faculty members in 1982.) Some years later, the head of another research institute in Washington said to me of DO, "Anyone can see it's a sick institution. Harvard is bleeding it white."

4 The then director of Dumbarton Oaks, Giles Constable, who had barely met me and had no professional competence in my field of Byzantine history and literature, was said to have described me as "a traitor to Harvard."

5 In this I am not alone. See Josiah Ober, "Letter from the President: Too Much Companionship?," *American Philological Association Newsletter* 32 (2009): 1–3, in which the president of the principal association of classicists announced, "I no longer accept invitations to contribute to classical Companions," by which he meant "multiple-author reference works."

6 Jencks and Riesman, *Academic Revolution*, 536.

7 Zachary Karabell, *What's College For? The Struggle to Define American Higher Education* (New York: Basic Books, 1998), 68.

8 Karabell, *What's College For?*, 71.

9 Making a related argument, Mark C. Taylor, *Crisis on Campus: A Bold Plan for Reforming Our Colleges and Universities* (New York: Alfred A. Knopf, 2010), 46–7, predicts, "Without radical changes, academic publishing will collapse in the near future." I find this unlikely, though I would welcome a sensible reduction in academic publishing.

10 Irina Andreescu-Treadgold and Warren Treadgold, "Procopius and the Imperial Panels of San Vitale," *Art Bulletin* 79 (1997): 708–23.

11 Warren Treadgold, "Predicting the Accession of Theodosius I," *Mediterraneo Antico* 8 (2005): 767–91 (accessible online at https://www.academia.edu/4780567/Predicting_the_Accession_of_Theodosius_I).

12 Cf. Victor Davis Hanson, John Heath, and Bruce Thornton, *Bonfire of the Humanities: Rescuing the Classics in an Impoverished Age* (Wilmington, DE: ISI Books, 2001), especially 195–203, describing Heath's attempts to publish an article he originally entitled "Genitives and Genitals: Self-Promotion and the 'Crisis' in Classics," which *Classical World* eventually published only after insisting on extensive revisions that were obviously motivated by ideology.

13 See the annotated reprints of these two articles with further commentary in Alan Sokal, *Beyond the Hoax: Science, Philosophy and Culture* (Oxford: Oxford University Press, 2008), especially 7 and 93 (with note).

14 See "Trouble at the Lab," *Economist*, October 19, 2013, 28; and "Academic Publishing: Science's Sokal Moment," *Economist*, October 5, 2013, 85.

15 This fact seems somewhat odd, because one might expect the unpublished books and articles to be worse than the published books, but probably many publishers reject their worst submissions without sending them to reviewers.

16 The book was Chris Wickham, *Framing the Early Middle Ages: Europe and the Mediterranean, 400–800* (Oxford: Oxford University Press, 2005).

17 My favorable opinion is doubtless somewhat influenced by my having received two NEH research fellowships myself and my wife's having received another, though my enthusiasm is somewhat curbed by the fact that neither of us has ever been asked to serve on the selection panels, as many former NEH fellows have been.

18 Lionel S. Lewis, *Marginal Worth: Teaching and the Academic Labor Market* (New Brunswick, NJ: Transaction Publishers, 1996), 64.

19 See Warren Treadgold, "Imaginary Early Christianity," *International History Review* 15 (1993), 535–45, and Treadgold, "Taking Sources on Their Own Terms and on Ours: Peter Brown's Late Antiquity," *Antiquité Tardive* 2 (1994), 153–9. Some of my book reviews are also of this type.

CHAPTER 6: PROPOSALS FOR LEGISLATION

1 See the discussion of these criteria on pp. 94–7 above. One prominent feature of most dissertations, the exhaustive listing of previous books and articles regardless of their scholarly value, should not be rated as such, though neglect of relevant studies should lead to lower ratings for accuracy and rigor.

2 Admittedly these junior employees would know the identities and institutions that they had redacted from the dissertations, but they, like the senior members of the board, should make every effort to be fair and recuse themselves in case of a conflict of interest (or at least disclose the conflict of interest to their colleagues).

3 This seems to have been the reaction of the editors of *Academic Questions* when they accepted an earlier version of this chapter as an article: "How to Hire Better Professors," *Academic Questions* 15 (2001–2): 39–49. See the editors' summary on p. 3 of this issue: "Warren Treadgold *imagines* a more orderly process" (italics mine).

4 Such is the somewhat surprising conclusion of Michèle Lamont, *How Professors Think: Inside the Curious World of Academic Judgment* (Cambridge, MA: Harvard University Press, 2009).

5 See, e.g., Sheila Slaughter, "Academic Freedom, Professional Autonomy, and the State," in Hermanowicz, *American Academic Profession*, 259–61.

6 See, e.g., Adam Marcus and Ivan Oransky, "Crack Down on Scientific Fraudsters," *New York Times*, July 11, 2014, A21.

7 See above, pp. 33–4.

8 See Arum and Roksa, *Academically Adrift*, 136–42.

9 See Stephanie Saul, "Big Jump in Million-Dollar Pay Packages Is Seen for Presidents of Private Colleges," *New York Times*, December 11, 2017, p. A12.

10 See Greene, "Administrative Bloat."

11 Bok, *Higher Education*, 111.

12 Bok, *Higher Education*, 110.

13 Keller and Keller, *Making Harvard Modern*, 367.

14 Bok, *Higher Education*, 85.

15 For a good description of such students, see Professor X, *In the Basement of the Ivory Tower: Confessions of an Accidental Academic* (New York: Viking, 2011), especially xvii: "This push for universal college enrollment, which at first glance seems emblematic of American opportunity and class mobility, is in fact hurting those whom it is meant to help. Students are leaving two- and four-year colleges with enormous amounts of debt.... For those of my students who want to become state troopers or firemen, the unnecessary cost and the inefficiency of the whole process is staggering."

CHAPTER 7: A PROPOSAL FOR A UNIVERSITY

1 See the figures compiled by the National Association of College and University Business Officers and Commonfund Institute (http://www.nacubo.org/ Documents/EndowmentFiles/2016-Endowment-Market-Values.pdf). (I omit the University of Texas System endowment [$24.2 billion] because it supports several universities.) After Harvard ($34.5 billion), Yale ($25.4 billion), Stanford ($22.4 billion), and Princeton ($22.2 billion), the next best-endowed universities are MIT ($13.1 billion) and the University of Pennsylvania ($10.7 billion). An endowment figure for Berkeley cannot easily be calculated from the endowments of the whole University of California ($8.3 billion) and the UC Berkeley Foundation ($1.6 billion), and in any case the endowments of public universities are not directly comparable to those of private universities as indicators of prestige.

2 The order, however, is different: Princeton ($2.6 million/student), Yale ($1.9 million), Harvard ($1.8 million), Stanford ($1.4 million). See Ben Meyers and Brock Read, "If Republicans Get Their Way, These Colleges Would See Their Endowments Taxed," *Chronicle of Higher Education*, November 2, 2017 (https:// www.chronicle.com/article/If-Republicans-Get-Their-Way/241659).

3 The University of Chicago, an important university though in my view less influential than Stanford (or Harvard, Princeton, Yale, or Berkeley), was founded a year earlier than Stanford, in 1890, with money from John D. Rockefeller and land from Marshall Field. Its current endowment is $7.0 billion ($0.5 million/student).

4 See Maya Dollarhide, "University Donations Hit a Record in 2015," *Investopedia*, January 27, 2016 (http://www.investopedia.com/articles/personal-finance/012716/university-donations-hit-record-2015.asp).

5 While Georgetown (with an endowment of $1.5 billion) is not a leading university as that term is used here, its current status as the best university in the Washington metropolitan area has given it an importance it would not otherwise have. The importance of George Washington University (with an endowment of $1.6 billion), the University of Maryland, and George Mason University has also been enhanced by their location in or near Washington.

6 Similarly, learning a computer language should not satisfy the language requirement, because any computer language used today will soon be obsolete, as Greek, Latin, French, and German will not.

7 A provost might become necessary later, if the university added a medical or law school.

8 Henry Rosovsky, *The University: An Owner's Manual* (New York: Norton, 1990), 286.

9 See above, pp. 94–7.

10 Though applicants might be reluctant to request the usual three recommendations for fear that their application to a controversial institution might become known, almost everyone has at least one colleague he can trust.

11 For example, at many institutions professors hired or promoted when money is short can be paid much less than inferior colleagues hired or promoted in a good fiscal year, and raises of equal percentages can make such differences permanent. Publishing a major book may result in a permanent raise of thousands of dollars in a good year but no raise at all in a year of a salary freeze.

12 See above, p. 65.

13 Female students at many universities where they now form a large majority tend to feel undervalued and pressured into having sex because the male students can easily find other girlfriends. (Conversely, when I was an undergraduate at Harvard when male students were the overwhelming majority, they often claimed that the female students were overbearing because they could easily find other boyfriends.) More nearly balanced numbers of men and women should diminish this problem.

14 For Harvard's recent efforts to destroy the identities of its houses, see Douthat, *Privilege*, 21–4. Despite some faculty opposition, the Harvard administration also wants to identify and punish students who join single-sex "final" clubs not affiliated with the university; see John S. Rosenberg, "The Fractured Faculty," *Harvard Magazine*, November 9, 2017 (https://www.harvardmagazine.com/2017/11/harvard-final-clubs-and-faculty-governance-challenges).

15 George H. Douglas, *Education Without Impact: How Our Universities Fail the Young* (New York: Birch Lane Press, 1992), 202, laments that various American attempts to recreate "something like the collegiate model of Oxford and Cambridge" have been frustrated by "standardized old-line departments," which he deplores. Those departments are however the basis of American education, and any effort to create units that circumvent them will probably circumvent academic interests along with them.

16 Cf. Lewis, *Excellence*, 79: "I have never met a dean with responsibility for [ethnic] theme dorms who would not have preferred to see them abolished, but they are politically difficult to eliminate once they are entrenched."

17 Cf. Lewis, *Excellence*, 67n: "It is an odd irony to think that Harvard should be

engaged in a competition with other universities to send away more students who have so eagerly sought to attend—especially since a number of colleges with robust study-abroad programs adopted them in part because of housing shortages, limited academic opportunities, or locations in sleepy towns that do not hold the interest of their students for four consecutive years."

18 On such committees, see Hacker and Dreifus, *Higher Education?*, 19–22.

19 Cf. Ginsberg, *Fall*, 121, summarizing judicial rulings on the subject and his own opinion, which is by no means that of a conservative: "The expression of words, symbols, or views that someone finds offensive is not harassment. Rather, it is constitutionally protected speech."

20 Fielding intercollegiate teams with any chance of winning games would require large expenditures and severe distortions of admissions, scholarships, and faculty salaries (for coaches, who often have the highest salaries on campuses).

21 By this I mean, for example, that a good specialist in Dante can usually teach all of Renaissance literature even if he cannot necessarily teach Victorian novels or Renaissance art. A good specialist should not be a narrow specialist, but everyone's knowledge is limited to some extent.

22 Martin Trow, *Twentieth-Century Higher Education: Elite to Mass to Universal*, ed. Michael Burrage (Baltimore, MD: Johns Hopkins University Press, 2010), 333.

23 Jencks and Riesman, *Academic Revolution*, 525.

CHAPTER 8: INSPIRING A RENAISSANCE

1 For a recent but disappointing treatment of the problem, which at least deserves credit for tackling it at all, see Eric Weiner, *The Geography of Genius: A Search for the World's Most Creative Places from Ancient Athens to Silicon Valley* (New York: Simon & Schuster, 2016), especially 13–63 (on ancient Athens) and 97–139 (on Renaissance Florence).

2 Published as a book, Treadgold, ed., *Renaissances Before the Renaissance: Cultural Revivals of Late Antiquity and the Middle Ages* (Stanford, CA: Stanford University Press, 1984).

3 This would still be true if, as is quite possible, the *Iliad* and *Odyssey* were composed by two different authors.

4 The five I consider great, all available in English translations, are Ammianus Marcellinus (ca. 330–after ca. 395), Procopius of Caesarea (ca. 500–ca. 554), Michael Psellus (1018–1078?), Anna Comnena (1083–ca. 1153), and Nicetas Choniates (ca. 1156–1217). If you doubt their greatness, as a sample I suggest reading Procopius's *Vandal War* (Books III–IV of his *Wars*), well translated by H.B. Dewing and Anthony Kaldellis in Prokopios, *The Wars of Justinian* (Indianapolis: Hackett, 2014), 144–250. For the historians in general, see Treadgold, *The Early Byzantine Historians* (New York: Palgrave Macmillan, 2007) and *The Middle Byzantine Historians* (New York: Palgrave Macmillan, 2013).

5 Bok, *Higher Education*, 358, quoted and discussed above, p. 33.

6 Such is Socrates's refutation of Protagoras in Plato, *Theaetetus*, 178.

7 See Colin McEvedy, *Cities of the Classical World: An Atlas and Gazetteer of 120 Centres of Ancient Civilisation* (London: Penguin, 2011), 42–52 (Athens) and 308–20 (Rome). For Florence, see C.-M. de la Roncière, *Prix et salaires à Florence au*

XIVe siècle (1280–1380) (Rome: Ecole française de Rome, 1982), 673–6.

8 For Bellow's response in the *New York Times*, see Saul Bellow, "Op-Ed: Papuans and Zulus," *New York Times Books*, March 10, 1994 (http://www.nytimes.com/ books/00/04/23/specials/bellow-papuans.html).

9 Euclid reportedly said when someone asked how he could profit from learning geometry, "Give the man a coin, because he must profit from what he learns."

10 For a more detailed discussion of such "innovative" scholarship, see Treadgold, "The Death of Scholarship," *Commentary*, December 2017, 29–33 (https://www. commentarymagazine.com/articles/the-death-of-scholarship/).

INDEX